Engaging
the
Enemy

Engaging the Enemy

LESLIE MONTGOMERY

LIFE JOURNEY®
Bringing Home the Message for Life

COOK COMMUNICATIONS MINISTRIES
Colorado Springs, Colorado • Paris, Ontario
KINGSWAY COMMUNICATIONS LTD
Eastbourne, England

Life Journey® is an imprint of
Cook Communications Ministries, Colorado Springs, CO 80918
Cook Communications, Paris, Ontario
Kingsway Communications, Eastbourne, England

ENGAGING THE ENEMY
© 2006 by Leslie Montgomery
Cover Design: Jeffrey Barnes

First Printing, 2006
Printed in Canada

1 2 3 4 5 6 7 8 9 10 Printing/Year 10 09 08 07 06

Library of Congress Cataloging-in-Publication Data

Montgomery, Leslie, 1967-
  Engaging the enemy : the Christian woman's guide to spiritual warfare
/ Leslie Montgomery.
     p. cm.
  ISBN 0-7814-4257-5
  1. Spiritual warfare. 2. Christian women--Religious life. I. Title.
BV4527.M59 2006
235'.4'082--dc22
                                    2005022094

To my children, Charlene, Jon, and Paul,
and to my grandsons, Jonathan and Dallin.
My prayer is that you will recognize the sacrifice
that was hard-won on Calvary on your behalf,
fight the spiritual battle at hand, run the race of life, and
win the ultimate and eternal prize that awaits you.

If you do not stand firm in your faith,
you will not stand at all.

—Isaiah 7:9

Contents

Acknowledgments

THANK YOU TO:

Dr. Ed Murphy, for your invaluable support, encouragement, and prayers. You were more helpful than I ever could have imagined. Thank you for going before me and clearing the thicket for me to be able to walk down a somewhat clear path. I couldn't have written this book without you.

Neil Anderson. Your wisdom and direction on this topic have inspired me and our conversations have fed my soul. I appreciate you.

The World Prayer Center and the worldwide intercessory prayer team. Countless people held my hands up in prayer through your ministry. Additionally, much of this book was written after spending hours on my face before God in the prayer closets at the center. Thank you!

Mary McNeil, my acquisitions editor and sister Princess Warrior, who believed in and was an advocate for this book because of her own passion for Christ and her desire for other women to walk in freedom. Your personal story of triumph inspires me daily.

Danny and Dale, my biological and spiritual brothers who God so graciously blessed me with. I'm so thankful God chose you to be my siblings. I love you. "Sissy."

Lori Austin, for your never-ending spiritual investment in this project and in me. Thank you for always looking at me through the eyes of Jesus.

Introduction

Books that leave an impact on those who read them are products of an author's passion. They are mirrors that reflect a hunger deep within, a product of the author's dreams, experiences, and desires. Such is the case with this book.

I was a baby Christian, only seven days old, when I stopped one Saturday morning at a yard sale near my home. The gentleman who was holding the sale had many books piled on a table. As I browsed through them, a specific book caught my eye. It was *The Handbook on Spiritual Warfare* by Dr. Ed Murphy. My heart raced, and I asked how much the book would cost.

"Fifty cents," the man stated nonchalantly as he sat behind the table, sipping his cup of java.

He explained that he was an announcer for the local Christian radio station and had received the book to review at no cost. The topic was "too controversial," so he was getting rid of it.

I dug through the bottom of my purse, found two quarters, and drove away, unaware of the treasure that I'd found.

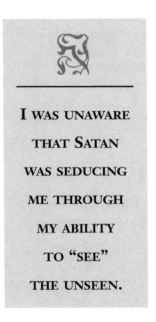

I WAS UNAWARE THAT SATAN WAS SEDUCING ME THROUGH MY ABILITY TO "SEE" THE UNSEEN.

Dr. Murphy's book was to have a lasting and profound impact on my life. *The Handbook on Spiritual Warfare* became like a second Bible to me. It would be instrumental not only in my life, but in the lives of thousands of others as I shared the principles it contained.

I have been deeply involved in the spirit world for most of my life. Unfortunately, my upbringing was far from Christian. Alcoholism, sexual abuse, paganism, and self-hatred occupied center stage in my young life. I was to follow this pathway of evil into my young adulthood, living in rebellion and idolatry.

As a young teen I read tarot cards for people. Others told me I had the "gift." Psychics and New Age leaders urged me to "submit" to unknown spirits. They said that in doing so I would become a great leader for the New Age movement that was rapidly spreading across America. I followed their advice, knocking on the door of hell and gaining access and information about how to hone my talent. I was unaware that Satan was seducing me through my ability to "see" the unseen.

My New Age mentors described the demonic guides to whom they'd introduced me as "harmless angels" or "spirit guides." We all assumed that these spirits were deceased loved ones, such as my Aunt Michelle, who died when I was eight years old. I was able to see events that others could not and to describe in intimate detail the events—past, present, and future—in the lives of others. The affirmation that I received because of my skills fed my empty, hungry soul and amazed my listeners. Demonic influences were leading me astray and were captivating others through what I saw and revealed to them.

"Grandma and Grandpa from California are coming to visit us," I once told my mother on a bright summer afternoon. We were living in Mountain Home, Idaho, and I was ten years old. My mother, though aware of my abilities, insisted that Grandma and Grandpa were not coming. Two hours later my grandparents unexpectedly drove their recreational vehicle into our driveway. Dreams and visions followed, as well as "feelings" of things that were about to occur. My abilities increased to the point that my mother asked me to stop telling her what was about to happen, insisting that she'd rather be surprised.

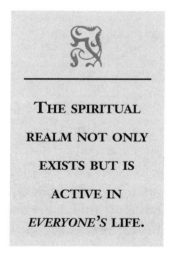

THE SPIRITUAL REALM NOT ONLY EXISTS BUT IS ACTIVE IN *EVERYONE'S* LIFE.

I attended a New Age church, spending hours a day in communication with spirit guides. My experiences included séances and contact with other psychics and channelers who shared my "gift." We called ourselves "white witches" who proclaimed good through "white magic." Little did I know that white magic is just as satanic as black magic. We enhanced our gifts through indulging in illegal drugs. I became increasingly entangled in a web of deceit.

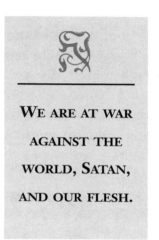

We are at war against the world, Satan, and our flesh.

Even though I was able to tell people about their pasts and futures, I was hopelessly confused about my own. While attending a country music convention, I met a man who was a believer in Jesus. He boldly shared his testimony about how God had delivered him from drugs, alcohol, and self-centeredness. He could see I was unhappy, unfulfilled, and spiritually lost. My deep need became evident to me, and I took the step of faith, trusting Jesus Christ as my Savior.

I was then twenty-five years old, a former slave of demonic forces who had become a servant of Christ. Shortly after my conversion I began to experience complete deliverance, and I learned how to renounce demonic strongholds in my life, replacing them with the strength of the Holy Spirit. Little by little every area of my life became submitted to Jesus Christ, producing healing and restoration.

Strangely, as I grew in Christ I noticed that other believers seemed to be threatened and skeptical about any discussion or acknowledgment of the spirit realm. I discovered there were even some born-again Christians who didn't believe in hell, let alone demonic forces. It was shocking and confusing to me. After all, the spirit world was as real to me as the air I breathed. I had undergone a radical change of perspective. Whereas I used to be on the *losing* team, I now saw things from the standpoint of the *winning* team!

I will forever be grateful for my "chance" discovery of Dr. Murphy's book. His work, as well as other books on spiritual warfare, has helped me to see that the spiritual realm not only exists but is active in *everyone's* life. Time and again they have taken me to God's Word, which clearly states that we are at war against the world, Satan, and our flesh.

The demonic strongholds that gripped me since childhood have released their grasp on my life. In their place is the peace, love, joy, and freedom available in Christ. The Lord has called me to share with others how to stand against the forces of evil.

This book is the product of years of intense personal study and collaboration with other ministry leaders. Its purpose is to equip you to walk in freedom.

There are many fine books that will teach you how to conduct a deliverance ministry, how to start an intercessory group, and even how to tear down the gates of hell on behalf of your city, state, and nation. *Engaging the Enemy* is a personal, practical guide to experiencing spiritual victory and freedom in your day-to-day battle with evil.

My prayer is for you to be strong, wise, and powerful, taking your stand in Christ and growing ever closer to him.

Our Identity:
Daughter and Princess Warrior

He destined us for adoption as his children through Jesus Christ,
according to the good pleasure of his will.

—Ephesians 1:5 (NRSV)

*E*very Christian woman needs to know who she is. In our culture today there exist numerous powers and influences that tend to cloud and confuse women's identity. Among the many destructive forces are divorce, sexual abuse, loneliness, financial difficulties, promiscuity, addictions, domestic violence, anger, lust, and gossip. These are just a few of the strongholds and difficulties we observe today in the lives of Christian women.

First Peter 5:8 warns us, "Your enemy the devil prowls around like a roaring lion looking for someone to devour." Indeed, he continues to devour many believers, enticing them to live outside God's will and spitting them out when he is through with them. It is tragic when believers live in defeat, especially when we consider that the battle has already been won at Calvary, providing the believer hope to overcome every trial, temptation, and sin.

Consider for a moment how you've dealt with difficult situations in your past. Did you fall apart or cave in to your circumstances? Did you become depressed? Suicidal? Did you become bitter and resentful? None of us handles every situation in a godly manner. But the choice to face problems God's way carries a promise. Romans 5:3–4 tells us that when we rejoice in our sufferings, it "produces perseverance; perseverance, character; and character, hope." We would sometimes prefer to forsake perseverance, character, and hope in pursuit of relief. But what if it were possible to attain the promise in Romans 5:4 *and* have relief? It is not only possible, but also readily available in Christ.

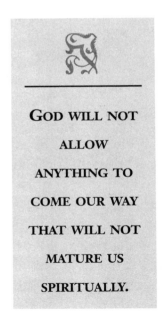

GOD WILL NOT ALLOW ANYTHING TO COME OUR WAY THAT WILL NOT MATURE US SPIRITUALLY.

BEARING THE EASY YOKE

Jesus said, "Come to Me, all you who labor and are heavy laden, and I will give you rest. Take My yoke upon you and learn from Me, for I am gentle and lowly in heart, and you will find rest for your souls. For My yoke is easy and My burden is light" (Matt. 11:28–30 NKJV). If his yoke is easy and his burden light, why is it so hard to deal with trials and tribulations?

When Jesus spoke of a yoke, he was referring to a piece of wood that rested over a person's shoulders to balance heavy loads. Many interpret this verse to mean that God will take our burdens away. In truth, he is saying he will make our burdens *chrestos*, a Greek word meaning "profitable for use in our lives in a moral sense." Jesus promises that God will not allow anything to come our way that will not mature us spiritually, as long as we cling to him. Our

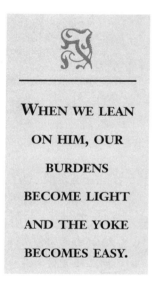

WHEN WE LEAN ON HIM, OUR BURDENS BECOME LIGHT AND THE YOKE BECOMES EASY.

perspectives and attitudes determine the spiritual outcome. We will either grow closer to God, or we will move farther away from him.

Jesus is "gentle and lowly in heart." He responded to situations with humility and gentleness. Every decision he made was in harmony with God the Father

THE DIFFERENCE BETWEEN BECOMING STRONG IN THE BROKEN PLACES AND BECOMING PERMANENTLY BROKEN LIES IN OUR GRASP OF OUR IDENTITIES.

and the Holy Spirit, which allowed him to rest. We will be able to rest when we trust that God knows how to deal with every situation in our lives. When we lean on him, our burdens become light and the yoke becomes easy because we know he is in control. He will resolve the situation in the way that best serves our spiritual development. (See Rom. 8:28.)

In his book *A Farewell to Arms*, Ernest Hemingway wrote, "The world breaks everyone and afterwards some are strong in the broken places." His words capture one side of spiritual warfare: Some people become stronger as a result of their trials. Others, however, find themselves weakened, depleted, and spiritually defeated. What makes the difference?

FINDING STRENGTH IN BROKENNESS

For believers, the difference between becoming strong in the broken places and becoming permanently broken lies in our grasp of our identities. It also depends on our ability to access the authority that flows from our identities, along with Christ's resurrection power.

Trials, tribulations, and suffering are inevitable. Many women, however, are either unaware of or unwilling to engage in spiritual warfare. The woman of God must cast off denial and ignorance, preparing herself for battle by utilizing the spiritual weapons Paul sets forth in Ephesians 6. We must "put on the full armor of God so that [we] can take [our] stand against the devil's schemes.... Therefore put on the full armor of God, so that when the day of evil comes, you may be able to stand your ground, and after you have done everything, to stand" (6:11, 13). We can't avoid the conflict, so we had better prepare for it.

THE POWER OF POSITION

The first tactic for blunting an attack is to gain an understanding of our position in Christ. Without this we disregard our worth and limit our capabilities. The world system is working hard to rob women of their value. Consider the thousands of children who are physically and sexually abused daily. Abortion clinics thrive. Our culture steals both the innocence and the faith of our young women.

As a daughter of the King, you are precious. Romans 8:29 says that God knew you and chose you to be his child before the earth's creation. Just as God set Jeremiah apart for a holy purpose (see Jer. 1:5), so also has he set

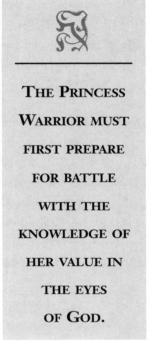

THE PRINCESS WARRIOR MUST FIRST PREPARE FOR BATTLE WITH THE KNOWLEDGE OF HER VALUE IN THE EYES OF GOD.

you apart. Psalm 139:16 says every day of your life has been preordained, written in your Creator's book. You are a chosen child of the King, the almighty and majestic Creator of the world.

Consider the very breath that gives you life. It comes from Almighty God. His breath oxygenates your blood, causes your heart to beat, and enables your brain to think. You cannot live without him. Do you understand that you are a daughter of the King and that his breath is inside you?

Perhaps you have experienced rejection from your parents and you find it difficult to believe that your heavenly Father could ever accept you. I understand. My own father rejected me when I was a young girl. He abused me and told me he wished I had never been born. The more I yearned for his acceptance and love, the more he rejected me.

Even as a young believer it was difficult for me to see myself as someone whom God valued. How could he love me enough to sacrifice his own Son for me? But I learned that I truly am a daughter of the King. He sees potential in me I had never before realized. He enjoys fellowship with me and offers me direction for every step of my life. He is the father I always wanted. He wants to be the same to you. But you must choose to accept him as your Lord and then embrace your identity as his daughter.

The Princess Warrior must first prepare for battle with the knowledge of her value in the eyes of God. She must understand who she was when she was apart from him. She must recognize who she now is in Christ. Colossians 3:9–10 says, "You have stripped off your old evil nature and all its wicked deeds. In its place you have clothed yourselves with a brand-new nature that is continually being renewed as you learn more and more about Christ, who created this new nature within you" (NLT).

My fellow Princess Warrior, recognize the esteem in which the Savior holds you. Embrace the identity that is yours in Christ. You are not alone. He has promised to be with you, never to leave you, and to lead you to the place of victory and rest. There is great power in knowing you are his daughter. But you are not *just* his daughter. Do you realize that you are also a warrior? An anointed *Princess Warrior.*

THE POWER OF A PRINCESS

Genesis 1:26 tells us God made us in his image, which is why the Bible places so much value on human life. When someone murders another person or aborts an unborn fetus, he is destroying an image

God created. According to the *Zondervan NIV Bible Commentary*, the word image, by definition, signifies a spiritual, intellectual, and moral likeness. In the Old Testament, the word image does not signify an exact duplicate, but only a shadow of the original, representing the prototype in an imprecise manner and lacking the essential characteristics of the original. While God created us in his image, we are neither an exact duplicate of him nor his mirror image. Second Corinthians 4:4 tells us that Christ is the image of God. Indeed, in this Scripture they are one and the same. God's image finds its reflection not in physical form but in Spirit or breath. Jesus reflects the Spirit of God, and Scripture admonishes us to be like Jesus.

We are like God in many ways. We can bless or curse. We are creative, and we long for relationship. We can discern right from wrong and are responsible for our actions. Our longing for a relationship with God reflects his desire for a relationship with us.

We assume the image of the object we worship. The word *image* refers to a mirror's reflection. We mirror the world's image when we reflect its morals, intellect, and religions. If you've ever been to a circus or carnival and stood in front of a "fun mirror," you've seen a distorted view of yourself. Similarly, the world gives us a distorted view of who we are and who we need to be. It tells us success, money, status, size, and honor make a person. But that is a lie. Only the word of God offers a clear image of who we are in Christ.

It is fascinating that, regardless of how abusive a biological parent may be, and regardless of how perfect the adoptive parent is, most children still want a relationship with their biological parents.[1] It is normal to seek knowledge and understanding of one's background. It helps us understand our identity. In the same way that we experience confusion over our families of origin, we forget who we are in Christ and repeatedly return to the "fun mirror" image that is provided by the Enemy. When we live by that distorted image we end up miserable failures. That is what happens when we seek our identities by gazing in the wrong mirror. We find our true identities in the Bible. If we want to know more about who we are as well as who we are becoming, we need God's Word.

A REAL PRINCESS BRIDE

The Scriptures refer to believers as the bride of Christ, his chosen, the redeemed and sanctified, and his children. Every believing woman is also a Princess Warrior. She is skilled in all aspects of war but uses her knowledge only when absolutely necessary. She is strong and secure in her identity, and she understands that real and enduring beauty is found in the heart of a woman. The Princess Warrior is aware of the resources at her disposal and is not afraid to call upon the army that awaits her command. She is wise and doesn't use a legion to fight a battle that requires only a few soldiers.

She is growing in love, compassion, and understanding. She knows how to be both firm and gentle. She's learning when to hold her tongue and when to speak.

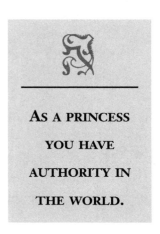

AS A PRINCESS YOU HAVE AUTHORITY IN THE WORLD.

She understands that by choosing her words carefully she can tear down a stronghold that would normally need the efforts of a hundred men, or she can be a balm to heal a broken heart. She picks her battles carefully, relying on her Father's knowledge and wisdom. She is loyal to him and sits under his counsel daily to expand her knowledge. She finds her greatest joy in the company of the King as they laugh together and enjoy one another's presence. She listens carefully to his advice and looks for ways to honor him in her decisions. She is, after all, a princess first and a warrior second.

Take a moment to close your eyes and consider how you picture a princess. What are her best features, and what is the foundation on which she stands? Let us now consider what God's Word says with respect to your identity as a princess.

First, a princess is a female member of a royal family. Scripture tells us God is your Father and King. Jesus, the Prince of Peace, is your brother. (See Mark 3:35.) Your lineage is royal.

Second, you are a princess who rules over a

principality. You have position, authority, and jurisdiction as a daughter of the King. You also possess, as a legal heir, all that is his. What is your principality? Your home, children, work environment, church, and more. What is your inheritance? Scripture tells us the righteous will inherit the earth and eternal life, as well as the new heaven and new earth. (See Ps. 37:29; Rev. 21:7.) Furthermore, 1 Peter 1:4 tells us we have an inheritance that will never perish!

Third, as a princess you have authority in the world. That authority enables you to move forward with confidence to use your gifts and talents according to Christ's will. Christ empowers you to overcome all difficulties in order to reach a specific group of people for his sake.

Next, Scripture identifies us as his bride. (See Rev. 21:9.) Matthew 25:5 describes Jesus as the Bridegroom. While the actual marriage will not occur until the second coming of Christ, the engagement at the time of conversion is a formal bond between the Bridegroom and the bride-to-be.

In biblical times, when a man and woman were promised in betrothal, a seal was made in the form of a dowry.[2] The dowry made the marriage legal even before the official ceremony. The bride was the owner of the dowry, and some have suggested that the dowry was an advanced inheritance from the bride's father. Similarly, as a believer you were given a dowry, a seal of promise, and a guarantee of your inheritance until Christ's return. (See Eph. 1:13–14.) The Holy Spirit is the down payment, providing you with both a foretaste of your spiritual inheritance and a legal claim to the fullness of the inheritance of the future. (See 2 Cor. 1:22.)

Jesus, the Bridegroom, has paid the "bride price" to the Father, who demanded justice for your sins through a blood sacrifice. You, in turn, have made the commitment to place God as the King of your life and to live your life according to his will.

> **HIS EXPECTATION FOR US IS TO BE NOT PASSIVE, BUT ASSERTIVE.**

Finally, you are a woman who possesses the honorable status and qualities of a princess. While the Lord has granted to you this status, it requires time and effort to develop your royal qualities. Your relationship with him will grow through prayer, reading and studying his Word, and ongoing fellowship with other believers.

Not only are you a princess, you are also truly a warrior, anointed and armed for battle on behalf of the King.

A WARRIOR CALLED TO BATTLE

You are engaged in a battle, regardless of whether you choose to acknowledge it. We are born into a spiritual battleground. That is why we are to "put on the whole armor of God" (Eph. 6:11 NKJV). He calls us to be "good soldier[s] of Christ Jesus" (2 Tim. 2:3). We daily face a battle for our minds, emotions, bodies, and spirits.

As a believer, you have taken on the cause of Christ and need to become assertive and enthusiastic in the spiritual warfare that is a part of everyday life. Most people think of spiritual warfare in defensive terms, but that is shortsighted. We must prepare for both an offensive and a defensive campaign. God, our Commander, calls us as soldiers to fight for the kingdom of Christ. His expectation for us, his Princess Warriors, is not to be passive, but assertive. Such was the case with a Princess Warrior who lived nearly 2,500 years ago and who took her stand in her understanding of her biblical identity, boldly stepping into spiritual battle for the preservation of her people. Her name was Esther.

Queen Esther:
A Biblical Example

*And who knows but that you have come to royal position for such a
time as this?*

—Esther 4:14

Queen Esther is an excellent example of a Princess
Warrior. When Esther was a child, her parents died,
leaving her as an orphaned Jewess. Her cousin,
Mordecai, took her into his home and raised her as
though she were his daughter. Considering her circumstances, Esther had ample reason to lie down and
give up, but she didn't. Instead, she drew near to God,
allowing the loss of her parents to fortify the faith she
would need for events yet to come.

Scripture tells us that King Xerxes sought to find a
queen to replace his wife, Vashti, who had dishonored

him by refusing to come before him when summoned. Her lack of respect led to her dethroning.
King Xerxes held a beauty contest to choose a new
queen. Mordecai entered Esther in that contest,
admonishing her to conceal her Jewish nationality.
Why? He knew Persian law stated that someone with
royal lineage must marry a wife belonging to one of
the seven great Persian families. Esther belonged to
none of them.

Esther obeyed her cousin and kept her nationality
a secret. After a year of preparation, Xerxes chose
Esther over all the other beautiful virgins and made
her queen of the greatest empire of that time. Susa
was one of the capital cities of a vast empire that
stretched westward from what is now India to Turkey
and Ethiopia. Esther co-ruled as queen over a great
amount of territory.

An Ancient Holocaust in the Making

Approximately five years later King Xerxes had an
ancient-day Hitler working for him. The man's name
was Haman, and the king had promoted him to sit
above all the other princes in the country. All the
king's servants bowed and paid homage to Haman—
all, that is, but Mordecai. While the custom of bowing
and paying homage to ranking members of the court
was common, Mordecai refused to do so. His loyalty
was to God alone. To bow before anyone else would
have been idolatry.

In response, Haman approached the king in an attempt to destroy not only Mordecai, but every Jew in the empire. He said, "There is a certain people scattered and dispersed among the people in all the provinces of your kingdom; their laws are different from all other people's, and they do not keep the king's laws. Therefore it is not fitting for the king to let them remain. If it pleases the king, let a decree be written that they be destroyed, and I will pay ten thousand talents of silver into the hands of those who do the work, to bring it into the king's treasuries" (Est. 3:8–9 NKJV).

The prospect of financial gain Haman offered was huge. Prior to marrying Esther, King Xerxes had fought and lost a costly war with Greece. The amount of money Haman was offering to the king was equivalent to two-thirds the value of the national treasury. How would Haman acquire such wealth? By plundering the wealth of the Jews. The king agreed to Haman's request to destroy the Jews.

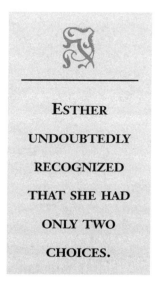

ESTHER UNDOUBTEDLY RECOGNIZED THAT SHE HAD ONLY TWO CHOICES.

After Mordecai received word that the wicked Haman had scheduled the Jews for genocide, he mourned in sackcloth and ashes, fasting, weeping, and wailing. Mordecai's official position at the king's gate gave him access to most of the royal compound, but not to the harem where Esther resided. Only when her maids and eunuchs informed her of his presence at the gate did Esther become aware of Mordecai's condition. In distress, she sent clean clothes for him to put on, but he refused them. She then sent her emissary back to Mordecai to find out why he grieved and would not be comforted.

Esther's attendant returned to her with the whole story of Haman's plot to annihilate the Jews and the copy of the king's decree that Mordecai had provided. They also brought a request from Mordecai to Esther to

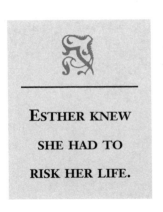

ESTHER KNEW SHE HAD TO RISK HER LIFE.

appeal to the king on behalf of her people. By law, however, not even the king's family could approach him uninvited. The penalty for such an offense was death. It had been thirty days since the king had called Esther into his presence. Esther was not expecting an opportunity to speak with the king any time soon.

A Heroine in the Making

Mordecai's communication must have chilled Esther's soul. He said, "Do not think in your heart that you will escape in the king's palace any more than all other Jews. For if you remain completely silent at this time, relief and deliverance will arise for the Jews from another place, but you and your father's house will perish. Yet who knows whether you have come to the kingdom for such a time as this?" (Est. 4:13–14 NKJV).

Esther undoubtedly recognized that she had only two choices: she could seek God and take action, which *might* result in her death, or she could do nothing and death would be *certain*. Esther's position as queen did not protect her from the decree that demanded her life. Neither did her position exempt her from the responsibility to act on behalf of God's people. Mordecai's timely question, "Yet who knows whether you have come to the kingdom for such a time as this?" moved the queen to act.

The Princess Risks Her Life

Esther knew she had to risk her life and violate court protocol. In her reply to Mordecai she said, "Go, gather all the Jews who are present in Shushan, and fast for me; neither eat nor drink for three days, night or day. My maids and I will fast likewise. And so I will go to the king, which is against the law; and if I perish, I perish!" (Est. 4:16 NKJV).

We might think this is where the spiritual warfare began. That is not the case. The spiritual battle started when Mordecai refused to bow to Haman. Haman's injured pride turned to indignation and resentment when he did not receive the honor that he expected.

Next, knowing that her life hung in the balance, Esther allowed the Lord to lead her to present her case to the king at just the right time. By entering the king's presence unbidden, the queen risked the loss of both her royal position and her life.

After three days of fasting and prayer Esther put on her royal robes and took her stand in the inner court of the king's palace, awaiting her fate. She had been faithful, and God honored her actions. When the king saw Esther, he showed her great favor and held out the golden scepter in his hand, inviting her to approach him. He said, "What do you wish, Queen Esther? What is your request? It shall be given you—up to half the kingdom!" (Est. 5:3 NKJV).

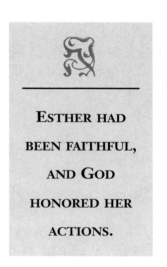

ESTHER HAD BEEN FAITHFUL, AND GOD HONORED HER ACTIONS.

Esther could have immediately petitioned for her life and the lives of her people. Instead, at the prompting of God, she wisely asked the king and Haman to attend a banquet she was preparing. Esther's servanthood and patience won the king's heart, and he agreed to go to her mystery banquet. At the banquet the king once again inquired, "What is your petition? It shall be granted you. What is your request, up to half the kingdom? It shall be done" (Est. 5:6 NKJV).

Once again, with the heart of a servant and waiting on God's perfect timing, Esther invited the king and Haman to attend a *second* banquet the following day. Consider for a moment why Esther would wait two extra days to plead for her life and the lives of her people. God was clearly leading her, teaching her his timing, and orchestrating the events in such a way that he would receive the greatest glory.

Haman's indignation toward Mordecai increased when he left the banquet and saw Mordecai at the king's gate. Mordecai neither rose to honor Haman nor showed any fear in his presence. Enraged, Haman ordered the construction of a gallows on which to hang Mordecai the following day. That same night King Xerxes suffered from insomnia.

GIVING GOD SPACE TO WORK

Esther had been faithful, and God honored her actions. He first arranged her invitation to the royal court, even though she had not been previously summoned. God also moved the king to spare her life. The Lord continued to bless her by afflicting the king with sleeplessness the night before the second banquet. We would not normally consider insomnia to be a sign of God's favor, but it was. God was ordering all things in order to prepare events for the following day.

The insomniac king kept his servants reading royal records to him throughout the night. The records revealed that Mordecai had at one time foiled a plot to kill Xerxes and had gone unrewarded. As the king pondered this fact, Haman entered the room to suggest to the king that Mordecai be hung. But before Haman could open his mouth, the king asked, "What shall be done for the man whom the king delights to honor?" (Est. 6:6 NKJV). Haman had no idea that the king was referring to Mordecai. His pride kicked into full gear, and he convinced himself that the king wished to honor him.

Haman answered the king, "For the man whom the king delights to honor, let a royal robe be brought which the king has worn, and a horse on which the king has ridden, which has a royal crest placed on its head. Then let this robe and horse be delivered to the hand of one of the king's most noble princes, that he may array the man whom the king delights to honor. Then parade him on horseback through the city square, and proclaim before him: 'Thus shall it be done to the man whom the king delights to honor!'" (Est. 6:7–9 NKJV).

The king agreed with Mordecai's suggestion and then ordered *Haman* to be the noble prince to array *Mordecai* and parade him on horseback through the city square. Imagine the expression on Haman's face! Haman followed the king's order with a sorrowful heart; then he attended Queen Esther's next banquet with the king.

At the banquet the king once again asked Esther, "What is your petition, Queen Esther? It shall be granted you. And what is your request, up to half the kingdom? It shall be done!" (Est. 7:2 NKJV).

The phrase "up to half the kingdom" was probably not a literal offer. It was a court idiom used by kings in the ancient Near East to indicate their generous disposition toward the person in view. In other words, the

king was giving great favor to
his wife and queen, Esther.

The queen answered and
said, "If I have found favor in
your sight, O king, and if it
pleases the king, let my life be
given me at my petition, and
my people at my request. For
we have been sold, my people and I, to be destroyed, to

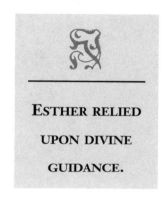

ESTHER RELIED

UPON DIVINE

GUIDANCE.

be killed, and to be annihilated. Had we been sold as
male and female slaves, I would have held my tongue,
although the enemy could never compensate for the
king's loss" (Est. 7:3–4 NKJV).

So King Xerxes said to Queen Esther, "Who is he,
and where is he, who would dare presume in his heart
to do such a thing?" (Est. 7:5 NKJV).

And Esther said, "The adversary and enemy is this
wicked Haman!" (Est. 7:6 NKJV).

JUST DESSERTS

The king was livid, and he left the room and entered the
palace garden. If he had followed harem protocol,
Haman would have left Esther's presence with the king.
Instead, Haman stood before Queen Esther, pleading for
his life, knowing death was certain.

When the king returned to the banquet from the
garden, he found Haman lying across the couch where
Esther was reclining (it was Persian custom to recline

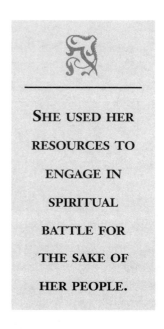

SHE USED HER RESOURCES TO ENGAGE IN SPIRITUAL BATTLE FOR THE SAKE OF HER PEOPLE.

during a meal). Although Haman was pleading for his life, the king thought Haman was assaulting Esther. Even as the word left the king's mouth, his servants covered Haman's face, and the king ordered Haman to be hung on the gallows that he had built for Mordecai.

At the conclusion of the story, Haman is hanging on a gallows, and the king has elevated Mordecai to the highest position in his court. Mordecai and Esther are authorized to write a new decree to save the lives of the Jews.

Esther relied upon divine guidance for every step of her crisis. She had submitted her thoughts, words, and actions to her God. In response, God gave her favor. She won respect and honor from her husband, and she became a spiritual heroine to her people.

AN EXAMPLE TO FOLLOW

Esther was a Princess Warrior. She had no earthly royal ancestry, but God called her to be his daughter, as well as the queen of the most powerful nation on earth. She also ruled a spiritual principality that extended as far and wide as King Xerxes' kingdom but specifically encompassed the Jews in this situation. As a spiritual daughter of the King and the wife of a king she possessed authority, and she used her resources to engage in spiritual battle for the sake of her people, the Jews, preserving them as a nation.

There are other ways that Esther fit the profile of a Princess Warrior. She accepted God's will, humbly submitting to his discipline and timing. She trusted in God's providence and responded to his call. God used her to accomplish his purposes. From an earthly and physical standpoint, Esther earned the respect of the palace staff, who in turn submitted to her leadership. Her influence was extraordinarily powerful and continues thousands of years after her death.

In the same way, God has called you to battle on behalf of others whom he has placed into your care. Sisters, read the following words—a paraphrase of Esther's cousin's words— carefully: Do not think in your heart that you will escape this battle any more than all other believers. For if you remain silent at this time, relief and deliverance will arise from another place. Yet who knows whether you have come to the kingdom for such a time as this?

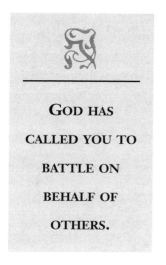

GOD HAS CALLED YOU TO BATTLE ON BEHALF OF OTHERS.

The Courtship of Good and Evil

Again, the devil took him to a very high mountain and showed him
all the kingdoms of the world and their splendor. "All this I will
give you," he said, "if you will bow down and worship me."

—Matthew 4:8–9

*S*atan first attacked Jesus immediately after his conception by the Holy Spirit in the womb of his mother, the virgin Mary. Matthew 1:18 records that Mary was pledged to be married to Joseph, but before they came together as husband and wife she was found to be with child through the Holy Spirit. Because Joseph was a righteous man and did not want to expose Mary to public disgrace, he had in mind to divorce her quietly instead. Without God's intervention and the pliable heart of Joseph, Mary would have been a single parent—an outcast in that day—raising our Savior. Satan often begins his courtship by attacking God's sanctified children at conception. Consider the number of miscarriages, abortions, premature babies, and childhood illnesses that occur on an annual basis. While all premature deaths are not the result of satanic attack, undoubtedly, many are.

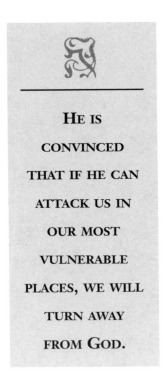

HE IS CONVINCED THAT IF HE CAN ATTACK US IN OUR MOST VULNERABLE PLACES, WE WILL TURN AWAY FROM GOD.

The next spiritual battle that Scripture records is shortly after Jesus' birth, when Herod sought to kill the Messiah. Numerous other assaults followed, from the Pharisees' jealous and arrogant actions to demons confronting Jesus as he performed miracles. There were attacks on him as he watched his friends and family experience life's heartaches and through the twelve disciples who deserted him in his greatest time of need. There was also his turmoil in the garden of Gethsemane and his anguish on the cross. Even though Mel Gibson's movie *The Passion of the Christ* vividly portrayed Jesus' physical anguish, there was no way it could adequately portray the spiritual battle. None of us will fully understand that aspect until we stand before our Maker.

THE ROOT OF SATANIC ATTACK

All of Satan's attacks stem from his desire to have power and control over God's creatures and creation. He is convinced that if he can attack us in our most vulnerable places, we will turn away from God and accept the lie that following the Evil One is the better way. A clear example of this is his attempt to seduce Jesus in Matthew 4. The Devil offered Christ the world in exchange for his loyalty, his spiritual inheritance, and his faith. Jesus, of course, declined his offer. Satan offers to us similar deals throughout our lives.

SATAN LEADS US BY A GOLDEN NOSE RING, ESCORTING US DOWN THE SHORTCUT TO ETERNAL DAMNATION.

Many of his offers seem particularly attractive to women. Why is that? Wealth and earthly treasure, success, and advancement represent power in today's society. Power leads to status. But all of this is temporary, "where moth and rust destroy, and where thieves break in and steal" (Matt. 6:19). Proverbs 10:2 describes such accomplishments as ill-gotten treasures with no value. Yet we strive for them even to the point of treating others

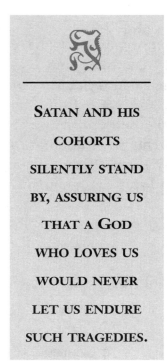

SATAN AND HIS COHORTS SILENTLY STAND BY, ASSURING US THAT A GOD WHO LOVES US WOULD NEVER LET US ENDURE SUCH TRAGEDIES.

viciously in order to acquire them.

Satan knew he was speaking to the Son of God, the firstborn of all creation, so he fired with both barrels—a direct frontal assault against Jesus. With us, however, he is generally more subtle in his attacks. He deceives us into thinking that we are simply determined to gain the same worldly treasures that everyone else wants. In our striving, however, Satan leads us by a golden nose ring, escorting us down the shortcut to eternal damnation.

Satan also tries to lure us to himself through abuse and pain. The lasting effects of his attacks on us when we are children become the basis on which he courts us as teens and adults. Those who have experienced childhood abuse, abandonment, false religions, and legalism often grow up defiant and angry toward God for allowing them to endure such hardships. Satan and his cohorts silently stand by, assuring us that a God who loves us would *never* let us endure such tragedies. They feed our feelings of abandonment, perfectionism, and self-hatred. The

Enemy of our souls—in an imitation of God's goodness—then promises to fill that void.

One of his most frequent strategies is to offer us internal peace. Internal peace is something we each desire. People often refer to their lack of peace as a "void" that they feel. Even believers sometimes try to find peace outside of Christ. One way is through overmedication. As a nation, we in the United States of America consume five billion tranquilizers, five billion barbiturates, three billion amphetamines, and sixteen thousand tons of aspirin every year.[1] Those figures are barely the tip of the iceberg when we also consider such substances as alcohol, nicotine, and various other over-the-counter substances. One reason twelve-step groups are so prominent in today's society is because of the obsession to find peace outside of God.

THE BATTLE FOR YOUR SOUL

A battle for your soul is taking place, and Satan will use whatever he can to deceive you into giving it to him. If you are an unbeliever, you are property that he is seeking to purchase.

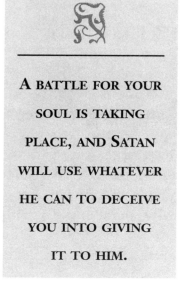

A BATTLE FOR YOUR SOUL IS TAKING PLACE, AND SATAN WILL USE WHATEVER HE CAN TO DECEIVE YOU INTO GIVING IT TO HIM.

"All this I will give you," he says, "if you will bow down and worship me." (See Matt. 4:9.) Satan, however, is not telling you the whole story. A fuller, more truthful offering would sound like this: "I will give all this to you if you will bow down and worship me, but only until Jesus comes back. He will at

GOD DOESN'T

COME TO US

EMPTY-HANDED.

that point utterly defeat me. Then, together with me, you will spend eternity in hell. You will live in the lake of fire prepared for the Devil and his angels, where there is weeping and gnashing of teeth. Your thirst will be unquenchable. You will remain in constant torment. But look at the

bright side. You'll have fun while you're here on earth. So how about it? I'll give you the world; you give me your soul. Deal?"

This is why Scripture refers to Satan, the Adversary, as "the deceiver." Jesus said that "he is a liar and the father of lies" (John 8:44). The New Testament also refers to him as a destroyer, accuser, and murderer. What fool would ever make a deal with someone possessing those characteristics? Then why spend eternity with such a being?

THE COURTSHIP OF CHRIST

When Adam and Eve sinned in the garden, they brought spiritual death into their perfect relationship with God. It's interesting to note that God took the initiative and went looking for them, even as they hid from him. Although they were the ones who caused the division by their disobedience, God pursued them. He also pursues us.

God doesn't come to us empty-handed. Despite our rebellion, he comes bearing gifts. He graciously courts us by his Holy Spirit, offering to raise us from death to life and promising freedom from the curse of our sin through the redemption of Christ Jesus. He courts and woos us by his Spirit, drawing us to Jesus.

The Holy Spirit is a gift of immeasurable power. Jesus referred to him as the "Helper" (John 15:26 NASB), or, in Greek, as a *parakletos*, one who is called alongside another to defend, encourage, and comfort. He is referred to as "the Spirit of Truth." He walks beside us, exposing our need for something more than the world can offer. God comes to us in the Holy Spirit with promises of eternal treasure. The difference between the courtship of God and the courtship of Satan is eminently clear. Satan is a liar and a deceiver. The truth is not in him. God, on the other hand, cannot lie. He is the personification of truth.

Throughout the Bible there are thousands of promises God makes to us, his children. God makes good on every promise he makes to believers. He does not lie, and he will fulfill every last promise for the believer who walks according to his will.

Just as Satan's names reveal his character, so do God's many names reveal the aspects of his character. He is our Shield, Protector, Creator, Avenger, Healer, Fortress, Deliverer, Rock, Refuge, Provider, Shepherd, and Redeemer.

For many years I dreamed of meeting Prince Charming, someone who would love me unconditionally, care for me, protect me, provide for me, and walk beside me. I have found him in Christ Jesus. He is my beloved and I am his. His banner over me is love. His presence sustains and refreshes me. He is all I've ever dreamed of and more. I will dwell in his presence forever. What more could a woman of God want?

The Spirit Realm

*The fundamental battle is between the father of lies
and the Spirit of truth.*

—Neil Anderson

From the day we are born until the moment we die, we are in a spiritual battle, romanced by good and seduced by evil. The courtship of Satan does not end with our conversion. The Evil One cannot steal our salvation, but he continues to try to turn our hearts toward him and to lure us away from our First Love. He tries to convince us that the one who paid the ransom for us has lied to us and forsaken us. Our spiritual adultery is his goal. He knows that if he can get us to take our eyes away from our First Love, we will become useless to God. There are only two camps in this spiritual war: God's camp and Satan's camp. There is no middle ground. In order for us to evaluate clearly where we stand in the spirit realm, we need to understand the purpose of the war itself.

HOW THE WAR BEGAN

Isaiah 14 speaks of a spiritual war that raged in the heavenly realm between Christ and Satan, whose name was formerly Lucifer, the "angel of light." Lucifer desired "to climb up to heaven and to place his throne above the highest stars … where he would sit like a king … he would be like God."[1] Many theologians, such as Kenneth L. Barker and John R. Kohlenberger III, have suggested that Lucifer's rebellion was born out of God's decision to create humans above the angels. But Lucifer would not have been satisfied simply to be above humans; he wanted to be above the highest stars, where he would be like God. In fact, Lucifer aspired to rule over God.

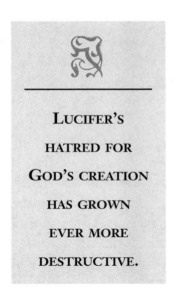

LUCIFER'S HATRED FOR GOD'S CREATION HAS GROWN EVER MORE DESTRUCTIVE.

Lucifer failed in his rebellion, and God evicted him from the heavenly realm. Since God placed human beings above the angels, including Lucifer, it is plausible to conclude that Satan's goal is still to destroy mankind. Furthermore, in his ongoing rebellion against God he attempts to wound God by destroying his most treasured creation: you and me.

Satan, after his expulsion from heaven, enlisted a hierarchy of angels (his followers) to carry out his evil plan to destroy God's children and the earth that they inhabit. Lucifer's hatred for God's creation has grown ever more destructive as, like a child who is out of control, jealous of a new sibling and angry with his parents, he continues to press the attack against God and his children. It began with Adam and Eve and continues today. God said in Genesis 3:15, "I will put enmity between you and the woman, and between your offspring and hers; he will crush your head, and you will strike his heel."

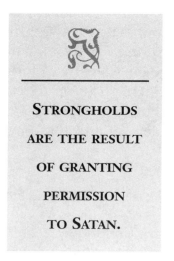

STRONGHOLDS ARE THE RESULT OF GRANTING PERMISSION TO SATAN.

THE WAR BETWEEN THE "SEEDS"

The focus of the previous verse is the conflict between the seed of the woman and the seed of the serpent. That battle will continue until the seed of the woman finally crushes the head of the serpent. The serpent will painfully bruise the heel of the woman's seed. When God speaks of the seed of Satan, his meaning is twofold: one seed of Satan is demons and evil spirits who are fallen angels and are like Satan in nature. The other seed is unredeemed men and women who bear Satan's nature. (See 1 John 3:8, 10, 12.) The twofold seed of the woman is the Lord Jesus Christ (see Gal. 3:16; Rev. 12:1–5, 13) as well as redeemed men and women who have accepted Jesus Christ as their Savior.

In Genesis 4 we see the first instance of the age-old opposition between those two seeds. It comes in the form of a satanic attack against the human family. Cain violently murders Abel, the seed of a woman. Satan has been unrelenting in his attacks against the human family ever since. He rallies his seed to attack, destroy, and kill woman's seed.

The Powers We Are up Against

By God's design, on the other side of the battlefield there is a hierarchy among God's angels, or the spirit beings that we know as archangels, messengers, warriors, and heralds. Scripture refers to fallen angels as rulers, authorities, powers, principalities, and spiritual forces. All angels, whether God's or Satan's, are active in the human arena, but neither side can act on its own authority. There must be permission from a spiritual commander—God or Satan—as well as a point of entry into the life of the human being who is under attack. It may take the form of a direct invitation or an opening that is the result of the permission of the human being who has spiritual authority over the victim, such as a parent. Demonic harassment can even take place through a generational entry point—that is, past demonic involvement in the family.

It is important to clarify here what we mean by demonic involvement as opposed to demonic possession. Satan cannot "possess" a Christian. Possession implies ownership. When an individual makes a commitment to receive Christ as her Savior, she becomes a slave of Christ, purchased by his blood. Satan has no power to snatch away someone who belongs to God himself. Believers can nevertheless harbor demonic strongholds in various areas of their lives. Such strongholds are the result of granting permission to Satan, through willful submission to sin, to assert his influence in our lives.

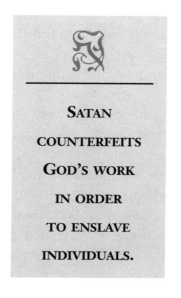

SATAN COUNTERFEITS GOD'S WORK IN ORDER TO ENSLAVE INDIVIDUALS.

As powerful as Satan may be, even to the point of establishing strongholds in the lives of believers, he is creatively impotent. He is not God, who alone is the Creator of all spiritual laws, principles, and structures that exist within the spiritual as well as the natural realms. In order to accomplish his purposes, therefore, he takes what God has already created for good and

HIS BLESSINGS SOON TURN TO CURSES.

twists it to his evil intent. Satan counterfeits and perverts the truth at every opportunity. He is a deceiver. Furthermore, since his forgeries have no value, his imitation of God's truth is short-lived. Lies are empty and unfulfilling. Still, Satan counterfeits God's work in order to enslave individuals. He is the original Jekyll and Hyde, masquerading as an angel of light to hide his true identity. But his blessings soon turn to curses, with darkness replacing the light and death consuming the life he has promised.

Fortunately, God's power is superior. Satan's is subordinate. God's power and Satan's are unequal. God limits Satan's power. Still, the Evil One is immensely powerful. The genocide that took place during the Holocaust provides ample evidence of the demonic influence and power one person who is sold out to Satan can wield. Over six million of God's chosen people died because one man, Adolf Hitler, willingly became a pawn of the Evil One. He led millions of human beings to cooperate with the satanic kingdom. The spirit world and the natural world are connected. What we do on earth yields spiritual consequences.

We can trace this all the way back to the beginning. Eve misled her husband Adam, who relinquished to Satan his position as lord of the earth. Adam and Eve lost their intimate relationship with God and were thrown out of the garden, the only place where the spiritual and earthly realms were in complete harmony. The choices we make affect our spiritual relationship with God and Satan, as well as our physical lives.

THIS PRESENT DARKNESS

We need only to drive into Las Vegas, New York, and New Orleans to sense a spirit of darkness. While witchcraft, prostitution, suicide, satanic worship, murder, and other hideous crimes are in every town, these cities emanate a blatant demonic presence. Even a hotel room in which ungodly activities have occurred can become a dwelling place for evil spirits. There are cities, towns, counties, and, yes, even entire states and nations in which the people residing in them have given themselves over to Satan. Strongholds begin with one individual who is willing to set aside God's will in order to fulfill his lusts. Like an infectious disease, this person travels to other receptive people until entire families and geographic regions become entrapped.

Nowhere was this more apparent to me than in a recent trip to eastern Europe. In 2004 I traveled to Budapest, Hungary, where I taught spiritual warfare

WE CANNOT SERVE OURSELVES WITHOUT TURNING OUR BACKS ON GOD.

principles to missionary parents and their children. The Iron Curtain had fallen years earlier, but the spirit of communism was alive and well in Budapest. The moment I arrived I sensed a spirit of oppression. It was evident in the way the city's inhabitants responded to one another and to the missionaries ministering there. Their attitude of hopelessness was manifested in everything, including their homes, attire, and faces. It obviously would take more than the falling of the Iron Curtain to set these people free.

KNOWING WHERE WE STAND

Before we can ever hope to set anyone free, however, we must discern where we ourselves stand. There are three symptoms that reveal the spiritual camp in which we are living:

1. Allegiance. To whom do we give our allegiance?
2. Obedience. Who are we obeying?
3. Relationship. To whom are we related?

When allegiance to Christ's kingdom, obedience to Christ, and a personal relationship with Christ are absent, the only alternative is to live in allegiance, obedience, and relationship to Satan. There is no middle ground. It must be one or the other. We cannot serve ourselves without turning our backs on God and facing the gates of hell. There are two commanders we can choose from, and we must decide whom we will serve and march forward in that calling. Luke 16:13 says, "No servant can serve two masters. Either he will hate the one and love the other, or he will be devoted to the one and despise the other." Matthew 12:25 tells us, "Every kingdom divided against itself will be ruined ... [it] will not stand."

Christians who sit astride the fence that separates God's kingdom and Satan's are in big trouble. They are married to Christ but flirt adulterously with Satan. Revelation 3:15–16 warns us, "You are neither cold nor hot. I wish you were either one or the other! So, because you are lukewarm—neither hot nor cold—I am about to spit you out of my mouth." Before a person ever involves herself in the battle, she must choose whom she will serve and not look back or consider the other side.

It was Joshua who called the Israelites to make a decision about their allegiances. He told them they must "choose [today] whom [they would] serve" (Josh. 24:15 NRSV). We have to make choices similar to theirs. I was sixteen when my older brother, Danny, joined the armed forces. Before choosing his branch of service, he considered the benefits of each. He carefully examined his life goals, his talents, and his needs. He then made his choice. Once he signed the paperwork, there was no turning back. In the same way, it is essential that each of us takes an honest look at the two opposing "branches of service" that we have to choose from and consider where they lead.

Have you made a life-defining choice in answer to the challenge to "choose today whom you will serve"? Where does your allegiance lie? To whom are you related? Who are you obeying? Be sure that you have made the right choice before you venture onto the field of battle. The battle is real. Satan wants to take you captive and destroy you. What he offers to you is a lie. His destiny is destruction. Jesus offers you fulfillment and life. The choice is yours: spiritual life or death, winning or losing.

The Dynamics of Battle

All those gathered here will know that it is not by sword
or spear that the LORD saves; for the battle is the LORD's,
and he will give all of you into our hands.

—1 Samuel 17:47

I do not believe there is "a demon behind every bush" waiting to attack innocent bystanders. There does not *need* to be, since there are two other enemies that are quite effective: our flesh and the world. Our flesh consists of the totality of our core beliefs, desires, and needs that, apart from Christ, are relentlessly self-centered. The world is comprised of millions of people who operate according to this fleshly standpoint. It is these two components—the flesh and the world—that since the fall have led to the moral deterioration of human beings and this planet.

Spiritual warfare is multidimensional, involving the world and our flesh, as well as demonic influence. Because our flesh demands fulfillment, we have become a society that is preoccupied with ourselves and unwilling to restrain our desires. We settle for Satan's counterfeits. Both our flesh and the world constantly badger our spirits to give in to their ways. And we do. This is evident in the media outlets of television and radio. Nearly every television sitcom and radio program that thrives today is centered on fulfilling our fleshly desires, from sexual immorality, homosexuality, and self-indulgence to self-exaltation, wealth, and pride.

WE CANNOT CONTROL THE EVENTS THAT HAPPEN IN OUR LIVES, BUT WE CAN LOOK AT THEM DIFFERENTLY.

Whether we are being attacked by the world, by Satan and his demonic cohorts, or by our own fleshly desires, we each follow the same basic cognitive mental process in our decision making. It looks like this:

1. We perceive an event with one of our five senses.
2. We have specific thoughts about the event; we reject it or justify it.

3. We experience any of a number of emotions.
4. We respond by choosing a course of action.

We go through this process, whether consciously or unconsciously, multiple times per day. Our understanding of it is vital to spiritual warfare because it will help us to sort out our motives, beliefs, and behaviors prior to taking action. Let's examine in greater detail each step of the decision-making process. We begin with the events of life that we perceive with our five senses.

OUR PERCEPTIONS

We can be upset over almost anything: our husbands working late, our children speaking disrespectfully to us, or our cars breaking down. It doesn't have to be a crisis. We cannot control the events that happen in our lives, but we can look at them differently. We must learn to analyze them objectively so that we can engage in battle with the appropriate weapon found in God's Word.

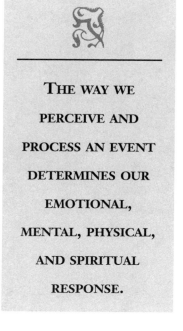

THE WAY WE PERCEIVE AND PROCESS AN EVENT DETERMINES OUR EMOTIONAL, MENTAL, PHYSICAL, AND SPIRITUAL RESPONSE.

Each person perceives events differently. Six different people can watch the same accident occur and recall it in six different ways. The same six people will have different emotional responses to events as well. Consider, for example, Vietnam War veterans. Two different men experience the same war and witness the same tragic events. One returns home with post-traumatic stress disorder. The other sails through life with no significant problems whatsoever. Why? It is because they have perceived events differently. The way we perceive and process an event determines our emotional, mental, physical, and spiritual responses.

Early childhood experiences and what we call "core beliefs" are often responsible for shaping our perspectives. Our core beliefs are the foundational beliefs on which we build our lives. Neil Anderson, in his book *Christ Centered Therapy* (Zondervan Publishing House, 2000), divides these foundational beliefs into five categories:

OUR CORE BELIEFS ARE BUILT ON OUR CHILDHOOD PERSPECTIVES OF VARIOUS EVENTS.

1. How we see ourselves
2. How we see others
3. How we think others see us

4. How we see God
5. How we think God sees us

These core beliefs are generally the result of events—real or perceived—that we experience during childhood or adolescence. One of the developmental stages that children go through involves the belief that the world revolves around them. When my infant grandson, Dallin, has a need, he cries. My daughter then meets his need, whether by feeding him, changing him, or simply holding him. As far as Dallin is concerned, the sun rises and sets because of him. This is a normal part of his development, and it will take a couple of years for him to realize that he is not the center of the universe. Children in this stage tend to internalize negative family events. The result can be guilt, shame, and a false sense of responsibility. We often carry these feelings into adulthood.

Our minds are like computer hard drives loaded with memories. If you were abused as a child, it is not the abuse itself that keeps you in bondage. Rather, what keeps you imprisoned are the lies or core beliefs about self and others that are the *results* of the abuse. Our core beliefs are built on our childhood perspectives of various events. Those beliefs change only when we confront them with truth and when, in faith, we choose to walk according to the truth.

When we were children we lacked the reasoning skills to defeat unhealthy circumstances, words, or actions that damaged us. Consequently, we were susceptible to negative core beliefs. Dr. Ed Murphy states, "If we have lies stored in our experiential knowledge we will have little choice but to act out

WITHOUT GOD'S INTERVENTION, OUR NEGATIVE CORE BELIEFS CAN CONTROL US.

accordingly or else live a life of constant struggle and self-effort. Mental darkness cripples the spirit; since we can only act as far as we can think, our spirit person (our real self) cannot live out its righteousness until the mind is free from unrighteous lies. Therefore, only when we purge our minds from lies can we live and act in the freedom of Christ."[1]

I grew up in a home with an abusive father and with a mother who was unable to stand up to him. There was no one to challenge my parents' behavior and to teach me why their behavior was wrong. As a result, I developed distorted core beliefs about men and women. I assumed that all men are abusive sex addicts, women are weak, and sex is bad. Although core beliefs can be true, they often are not. These core beliefs were formed in an abusive environment, and I held them for many years. Without God's intervention, our negative core beliefs can control us, sending us in a downward and destructive spiritual spiral.

When we consistently respond negatively to the same situation, we must take a mental inventory of our core beliefs. We need to pause and ask ourselves, "What might this look like from a spiritual perspective? Could it be a spiritual attack? Temptation? Trial?" If so, we should identify the biblical truth that speaks to our negative core beliefs. We must remember that we are not human beings in a spirit world, but spirit beings in a human world. Let us arm ourselves with that new perspective.

Part of that arming process is recognizing why Satan hates us. He hates us because of who we are in Christ. His desire is to make us ineffective in our walk with Christ. He will do everything possible, within the limits God sets, to mislead, distract, and harm us. We can, therefore, *expect* him to attack us. That will keep us from being shocked, traumatized, or immobilized when it occurs. Instead, we'll be prepared to fight back by knowing and standing on the Word of God.

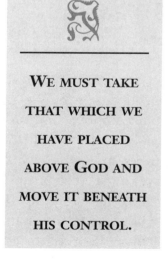

WE MUST TAKE THAT WHICH WE HAVE PLACED ABOVE GOD AND MOVE IT BENEATH HIS CONTROL.

It is not always easy to recognize negative core beliefs in our own lives because the primary strategy of the Enemy is deception. Unlike temptation and accusation from the

Enemy, deception is subtle. Satan misleads and misdirects us to believe a lie to be the truth. Satan deceived Eve. She believed what he was telling her, and the deception yielded disastrous consequences for her and all her descendants. If you are having difficultly identifying specific negative core beliefs in your life, you may want to petition the help of a Christian counselor, pastor, or mature believer to help you.

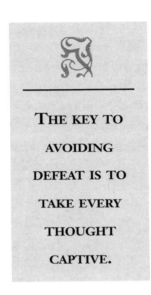

THE KEY TO AVOIDING DEFEAT IS TO TAKE EVERY THOUGHT CAPTIVE.

It is important to recognize negative core beliefs because they affect our thoughts. When we recognize them we take the first step in establishing the foundation of repentance and reshaping our core beliefs. We begin by admitting that we have been deceived. We must take that which we have placed above God, move it beneath his control, and place him back on the throne where he belongs. In order to live and walk in core beliefs based on truth, we must recognize that Jesus is truth (see John 14:6), his Word is truth (see 17:17), the Holy Spirit will guide us into all truth (see 16:13), and the truth will set us free (see 8:32).

The next step in the process of making decisions is to address the way we think about the events we have perceived.

Our Thoughts

Crisis, conflict, and difficult circumstances are inevitable. People in crisis tend to show poor judgment, act recklessly, get angry, and become argumentative. The way we respond to any given event will direct our lives for better or worse. One type of event to which we must learn to respond properly is temptation.

Each of us experiences temptation. Temptation is an "enticement to sin" that arises from human desires and passions. (See James 1:14; 1 John 2:16.) Enticement may also be from the Devil, who is called the tempter. (See Matt. 4:3.)

The Bible teaches that God does not tempt us. (See James 1:13–15.) He does, however, allow us to be tested by circumstances and by the Enemy of our souls. Such testing helps us to grow in our obedience, in our reliance on him, and in our commitment to his cause. The Lord also promises to provide a way of escape and will not allow us to be tempted beyond what we are able to bear. (See 1 Cor. 10:13.) When we resist the tempter, he flees from us. (See James 4:7.)

The key to avoiding defeat is to take every thought captive and make it obedient to Christ (see 2 Cor. 10:5) before we respond to any given event. That requires us to reframe our core beliefs. Our thoughts are the result of negative core beliefs we have retained from previous experiences, or they may be a result of words or pictures Satan places in our minds.

There is a battle raging in our minds between God's truth and our distorted core beliefs. We find victory by taking every thought captive to Christ, which means to submit our actions and thoughts to his truth. To submit ourselves is to place ourselves under the authority of another. In order to do that, we must first acknowledge the lie or idol that has captivated our minds. We can then confess and renounce the lie, accepting the truth of what God has said. How does this work in real life?

Consider my old core beliefs about men, women, and sex. In order for me to heal from my negative core beliefs, I had to first understand and embrace what God said in his Word about those subjects. Then I had to renounce the lie, or negative core belief, and continually repeat the truth that I had just learned. In doing so, I was bombarded by thoughts from hell, the media, and my own flesh, which still felt the pain of abuse. I had to do what the apostle Paul counsels in Philippians 4:8: "Whatever is true, whatever is noble, whatever is right, whatever is pure, whatever is lovely, whatever is admirable—if anything is excellent or praiseworthy—think about such things." That is not to say that we rid ourselves of negative thoughts simply by ignoring them. Rather, we let Christ's peace rule in our hearts by letting the words of Christ dwell richly within us. (See Col. 3:15–16.) We

WE OVERCOME LIES BY CHOOSING TO FOCUS ON THE TRUTH.

overcome lies by choosing to focus on the truth so that it replaces the negative thoughts or core beliefs.

Throughout this process we must remain alert to a serious roadblock: our own desires. Sinful desire feeds on pain and selfishness. James 1:14–15 tells us, "Each one is tempted when, by his own evil desire, he is dragged away and enticed. Then, after desire has conceived, it gives birth to sin; and sin, when it is full grown, gives birth to death."

The word *desire* is used to translate a Greek word, *epithymia,* that means "forbidden or unrighteous desires." (See Mark 4:19; John 8:44; Rom. 6:12; and Rom. 7:7–8.) It is often an impulsive craving and an ardent pursuit of what is forbidden. Another term for it is *lust*.[2] Our desires have the power to lead us down a pathway of trouble and death. We can recognize desire when we notice ourselves trying to justify thoughts that are contrary to God's Word. Desire can even motivate us to rip God's Word out of context, misinterpret it, and justify any sin. I recently heard a homosexual priest who was advocating same-sex marriage say, "The Bible talks about an intimate relationship between David and Jonathan. David said he loved him closer than a brother. They were sexually involved." That priest correctly noted that David loved Jonathan but incorrectly interpreted their love as a homosexual relationship, which the Bible expressly forbids. The priest was reading his own meaning into God's Word in an attempt to justify his own sinful desire.

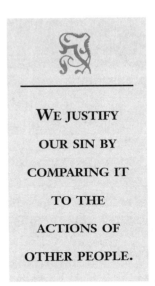

WE JUSTIFY OUR SIN BY COMPARING IT TO THE ACTIONS OF OTHER PEOPLE.

One can only imagine the battle between truth and lies that was taking place in the soul of that priest. We may attempt to justify our sin, but the Holy Spirit will not let us so easily get away with that self-deception. He will make the believer wrestle in his spirit until he is willing to call sin what it is—sin. This internal turmoil is often what leads believers either into the counseling office for help or into the hospital for treatment of the resulting illnesses. Many sick individuals (whether mentally, emotionally, spiritually, or physically) are people who are ill because of their own sin!

Another way that we justify our sin is to minimize it. We might say, "Oh, it isn't a lie. It's partly true," "It's just a little white lie," or "It's no big deal." I've even heard married women justify flirting with someone other than their spouses. "It's OK to flirt with someone as long as I don't go any further." A friend of mine once attempted to justify his flirting with the cliché "I can look at the menu; I just can't order from it."

I used his menu analogy to challenge him. "What happens when you are physically hungry and you look at a menu?" I asked. "Your mouth starts watering, your craving to satisfy your hunger intensifies, and sooner or later you cave in to that desire."

My friend ignored my concern, and within three months he was in an adulterous relationship, separated from his mate, and filing for divorce with the intention of marrying his lover. He moved in with the other woman for six months before discovering that *she* was cheating on *him*. They broke up. He went back to his spouse, begging for her forgiveness and seeking reconciliation. But the damage was too great. My friend lost his spouse, the custody of his children, and his self-respect and integrity. He was guilty of minimizing his behavior, which led him into a web of self-deception.

A third way we justify our sin is by comparing it to the actions of other people. We say, "Well, I might gossip a little, but not as much as Susan" or "Well, he cheated on me. I never cheated on him. So what if I kissed another guy? At least I didn't cheat!" We must regard our sin in light of the Bible, God's standard, not worldly or human standards. Just because others cheat on their taxes does not give us the right to do so. Sin is sin and always produces negative consequences: separation from God, our eternal lifeline. We must, therefore, learn what the Bible says about our circumstances and bring our thoughts into submission to God's truth.

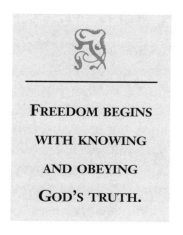

FREEDOM BEGINS WITH KNOWING AND OBEYING GOD'S TRUTH.

Only then will we be able to resist the Devil. (See James 4:7.) If we try to resist the Devil without first submitting to God, the Enemy of our souls will chew us up and spit us out. Jesus said, "If you hold to my teaching, you are really my disciples. Then you will know the truth, and the truth will set you free" (John 8:31–32). Freedom from the attacks of Satan, the world, and our own desires begins with knowing and obeying God's truth.

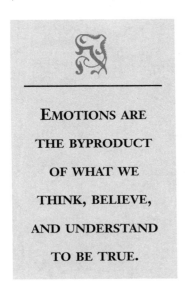

EMOTIONS ARE THE BYPRODUCT OF WHAT WE THINK, BELIEVE, AND UNDERSTAND TO BE TRUE.

Once we have taken our thoughts captive, we begin to resist the Devil. He does not have control over us. Actively choosing to bind our thoughts and hold them accountable to God's Word gives us the upper hand over the lies of the Enemy. The battle dynamic of taking our thoughts captive is crucial because our emotions and responses follow our thoughts.

Our perceptions and our thoughts are only part of the equation. We also must consider our emotions. The way we feel about our experiences deeply influences our cognitive process.

OUR EMOTIONS

The word emotion comes from the Latin word *emovïre,* meaning literally "to move or displace." Emotions arise from mental stimuli or thoughts that have a symbolic meaning to the person experiencing them. Those symbolic meanings then lead to an action. Researchers

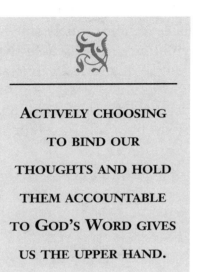

ACTIVELY CHOOSING TO BIND OUR THOUGHTS AND HOLD THEM ACCOUNTABLE TO GOD'S WORD GIVES US THE UPPER HAND.

generally identify twelve fundamental emotions, nine unpleasant and three pleasant[3]:

Unpleasant	**Pleasant**
Sorrow	Love
Fear	Joy
Anger	Awe
Jealousy	
Shame	
Disgust	
Pain	
Confusion	
Emptiness	

Emotions are the byproduct of what we think, believe, and understand to be true. When I was a child, my father would slap me on the backside and tell me that I was fat. In reality, I was a normal size for my height and age. But I chose to believe what he said and developed an image of my body that agreed with him. My reasoning skills were not mature enough to dismiss such inappropriate comments. I therefore began to swing like a pendulum, back and forth, between obesity and thinness achieved through bulimia.

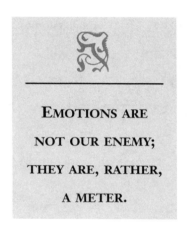

EMOTIONS ARE NOT OUR ENEMY; THEY ARE, RATHER, A METER.

My father's comments, along with other developmental issues, crippled my identity and self-esteem. I emotionally ricocheted among self-hatred, anger, bitterness, and a longing to die. My physical responses included self-mutilation, multiple suicide attempts, substance abuse, and sexual promiscuity. What was causing this? My emotions were responding to negative thoughts. I regarded myself as unattractive, worthy of rejection, and unworthy of love.

It has been said that our emotions lie to us; therefore, they cannot be trusted. But that is not really the case. What lies to us is our *thoughts*. Emotions flow from the core of our being, and they reflect the wonder of our creation in the image of God. (See Gen. 1:27.) Emotions are not our enemy; they are, rather, a meter that alerts us to things that are going on in our minds. God himself expresses a wide range of emotions. He is a passionate God and feels grief when we rebel. He is angry when we make idols of our

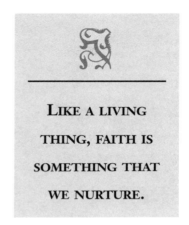

LIKE A LIVING THING, FAITH IS SOMETHING THAT WE NURTURE.

possessions. God delights when we return to him. Because we are made in his image, we also experience those feelings.

Jesus experienced a wide variety of emotions. He felt compassion when he met a leper and when a funeral procession passed by. He felt love when a rich young ruler came to him, anger when the disciples tried to keep little children from him, grief at the time of Lazarus's death, and deep sorrow over the unbelief of his own people, the Jews.

We too experience a wide range of emotions. Unfulfilled dreams and loss inevitably create emotional pain. Consider Hannah, who in First Samuel 1 had a loving and devoted husband but experienced pain because of her deep yearning for a child. Scripture tells us that she wept, restricted her appetite, and was depressed (1:7). She experienced "bitterness of soul" and "grief" (1:10, 16). But Hannah cried out to her God and shared her sorrow

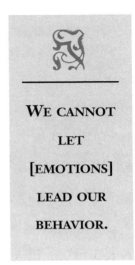

WE CANNOT LET [EMOTIONS] LEAD OUR BEHAVIOR.

with him and with Eli, the priest who stood nearby. Eli then, in turn, invoked God's blessing on her—a blessing that God fulfilled by granting her a child.

Our emotions are an important part of who we are, but we cannot let them lead our behavior as if we were driving without a map! The directions we must use are in God's Word. Without the intervention of taking our thoughts captive, we will repeatedly replay old "tapes" from our early childhood, causing our emotions to flare up like an open flame on which we pour gasoline. Some say that women are more emotional or sensitive than men. If this is true, it is vital that we hold our emotions in check so that we don't experience life as if we were on a roller coaster. Furthermore, if we don't learn this process now, imagine what it will be like when we go through the inevitable hormonal changes.

The way we perceive events affects the way we think, which produces any number of a dozen basic emotions. The final component in the cognitive process is our response—the course of action we choose to take.

Our Response

Our response to any given situation is in direct correlation to our emotions. *Feelings* are to *response* as *steering wheel* is to *car*. We may not initially recognize the cycle of thought, emotion, and response that leads to our behavior, but it is something we can learn. I grew up in a home in which my father was repeatedly unfaithful to my mother. I was aware of his many infidelities. People gossiped about his behavior. For a time one of his lovers even shared my bedroom with me. In turn, one of the core beliefs that formed in me was that all men are unfaithful and unworthy of trust.

That core belief stayed with me, even later in life after I had married. Any time my husband was late from work or absent when I thought he should be home, even when he was simply having lunch with a male friend, I accused him of infidelity. I spent hours crying and dwelling on the belief that he was cheating. After all, every man cheats, right? But he never did. How was I able eventually to move beyond this cycle of defeat and into a cycle of success? It was through the teachings of Scripture.

The Bible's instruction concerning freedom through spiritual warfare is based on the word *stand*. Consider the following verses:

> Watch, *stand* fast in the faith, be brave, be strong. (1 Cor. 16:13 NKJV)

Stand firm and you will see the deliverance
the LORD will bring you today. (Ex. 14:13)

You will not have to fight this battle. Take up
your positions; *stand* firm and see the deliverance the LORD will give you. (2 Chron. 20:17)

He lifted me out of the slimy pit, out of the
mud and mire; he set my feet on a rock and
gave me a firm place to *stand*. (Ps. 40:2)

If you do not *stand* firm in your faith, you
will not stand at all. (Isa. 7:9)

Therefore ... *stand* firm. Let nothing move
you. (1 Cor. 15:58)

Be on your guard; *stand* firm in the faith; be
[women] of courage; be strong.
(1 Cor. 16:13)

It is for freedom that Christ has set us free.
Stand firm, then, and do not let yourselves be
burdened again by a yoke of slavery. (Gal. 5:1)

Therefore put on the full armor of God, so
that when the day of evil comes, you may be
able to *stand* your ground, and after you have
done everything, to *stand*. *Stand* firm then.
(Eph. 6:13–14)

So then ... *stand* firm and hold to the teachings we passed on to you. (2 Thess. 2:15)

> You too, be patient and *stand* firm, because
> the Lord's coming is near. (James 5:8)

And Now We Stand

In order to "stand," we must have faith, which is the ability to live believing that God has told the truth. The movie *Simon Birch* tells a wonderful story about faith. Simon, the main character, is an unusually small boy born with a weak heart. He is not expected to survive infancy, but Simon surprises everyone and lives. Simon firmly believes that God has given him life for a reason, a purpose that only he can fulfill. As the story unfolds, Simon searches until he finally discovers his destiny.

But the odds are against Simon. Not only is he small in stature and physically deformed, but his parents and most of society have no use for him. Throughout the movie, Simon is taunted and teased by his peers and adults. Everyone from his pastor to his best friend warns him to stop believing in his fantasy of a divine purpose. But Simon remains convinced. He can't explain *how* he knows that God has a plan for his life. He just knows it. He is convinced that he's an instrument of God.

Simon's faith eventually leads him to the fulfillment of his life purpose. Everyone realizes that Simon has a God-given purpose that he fulfills in a unique way.

At one point Simon says, "I don't need proof [of God's plan]. I have faith." Faith is something that we have. Scripture does not tell us to find or create our

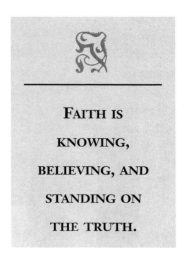

FAITH IS KNOWING, BELIEVING, AND STANDING ON THE TRUTH.

faith, but rather to build our faith. (See Luke 17:5.) We build on something that we already possess. Like a living thing, faith is something that we nurture, and it grows. If we neglect faith, it withers and dies. Sadly, circumstances can tear down our childlike faith before it has the opportunity to flourish.

How does faith grow? Faith develops as we put our trust in an authority that demonstrates reliability and consistency. That is why children believe in Santa Claus and the Easter Bunny. Our parents tell us stories about characters, and since we view our parents as reliable authorities, we believe them. Our parents may also teach us that Jesus loves us, died for us, and will never forsake us. But as we grow and mature, we learn that there is no Santa, no Easter Bunny, and no fairy godmother. We may feel as if our parents have deceived us. If Santa is a fairytale, then maybe Jesus is too. We may begin to challenge Jesus' existence—is he a real historical figure or just a fictional character? Parents seldom realize how they deplete a child's faith with stories that are based on fantasy rather than truth. Faith is nurtured with consistent truth.

Faith is knowing, believing, and standing on the truth even when circumstances or feelings suggest otherwise. Knowing is different than wondering. The foundation of spiritual warfare is knowing the truth. We know the truth because the Bible tells us and then God confirms it through the Holy Spirit. If the Bible says it, then we believe in faith that it is true. If it is true, then we stand on it—regardless of our circumstances or feelings. When we use the Bible as God intended, it brings healing, hope, encouragement, and trust as the Holy Spirit comforts, teaches, and guides us.

If we do not believe the Bible to be true, then we cannot be born again and will live in an ongoing cycle of defeat. If we have doubts about the Bible, we will be unable to press on in the midst of spiritual warfare. Accepting Jesus as our Savior is predicated on the knowledge that God's Word is true, that Jesus died for us, that he has forgiven us, and that he has a plan for us. Without faith in these realities, we cannot believe. If we do not believe, it is because we do not trust that what God has said is true.

Belief + Trust = Faith

We must have faith like Simon Birch, believing that God has a plan of spiritual success for our lives—a plan that includes living the life of freedom. That plan is available in a simple, understandable blueprint called the Bible. If we stand in faith on what the Bible says, then despite what our flesh and the world might say, *all* things are possible for us.

Faith heals, motivates, and cleanses. It moves mountains, breaks chains of demonic captivity, provides for our every need, and—most important—gives us eternal life. Faith is something that my eldest grandson, Jonathan, exercises whenever he stands on the couch while I encourage him to jump into my arms. I step back, open my arms wide, and say, "Go, Jonathan, jump into Grammy's arms!" He reacts immediately, knowing that I will catch him just as I have always done. He bends his little knees, extends his arms, and springs off the couch into my arms with a trail of laughter following him. In the same way, we put our faith into action because we know that God is able and willing to "catch" us.

Putting faith into action is not easy for many people. When I was growing up, I would have hesitated to "jump," because there were times when *no one* was there to catch me. My father played emotional mind games with me that led to mistrust. He would catch me only *sometimes*. He would then tell me that the bumps and bruises, cuts and scars would make me stronger and self-reliant and that I could depend on no one but myself. His "lessons" bred doubt, insecurity, and a lack of faith. But God doesn't play such games. With arms open wide he promises, "I am here, waiting for you. It is safe to jump into my arms. I will not let you fall. I promise. I give you my Word."

Smith Wigglesworth once said:

> God wants to sweep all unbelief from your
> heart. He wants you to dare to believe his
> Word. It is the Word of the Spirit. If you allow
> anything to come between you and the Word,

> it will poison your whole system, and you will
> have no hope. One bit of unbelief against the
> Word is poison. It is like the Devil putting a
> spear into you. The Word of Life is the breath
> of heaven, the life-giving power by which
> your very self is changed. By it, you begin to
> bear the image of the heavenly one.[4]

The Enemy has disabled many of us with his spear of unbelief. We find the power to heal that injury in God's Word. Will we begin to use its magnificent power? Or will we remain disabled, hopeless, and ineffective? We must discover the faith that is "the substance of things hoped for, the evidence of things not seen" (Heb. 11:1 NKJV). Things that we hope for and have not yet seen are visions for the future. The invisible is more real than the visible. Faith is the foundation of all things in Christ, including spiritual warfare. We must not let life's circumstances ship-wreck our faith. We can trust, we can believe, and we can walk in faith. Let us ask the Lord this very moment to increase our faith, remembering that "faith comes by hearing, and hearing by the word of God" (Rom. 10:17 NKJV).

EXAMPLES OF COGNITIVE PROCESS

An examination of positive and negative examples of the cognitive process will help us recognize the underlying reasons for our own defeat or success in the spirit realm.

Event: Your husband comes to bed late after working all day. You are in the mood for a little tender loving care. He says, "Not now."

FLESHLY EXAMPLE OF PROCESS	GODLY EXAMPLE OF PROCESS
THOUGHT:	*THOUGHT:*
He's not attracted to me anymore.	He's worked hard all day; he is tired.
He's having an affair.	He has a lot on his mind right now.
He thinks I'm fat.	He needs time to get sleep and recharge.
FEELINGS:	*FEELINGS:*
Anger, hatred, jealousy, bitterness.	Understanding, appreciation, empathy, love.
RESPONSE:	*RESPONSE:*
Roll over in disgust.	Offer a backrub to help him relax.
Give him the silent treatment.	Hold him, reassuring him.
Refuse TLC next time he wants it.	Approach him later for TLC.

Can you see the difference in the potential outcome based on the different thought processes? In the fleshly example, what core belief might lead you to believe that your husband is not attracted to you anymore, that he's having an affair, or that he thinks you're fat? Before you blame him, look deeper. Is that a core belief that you've had from childhood? Take those thoughts captive unto Christ and look at the circumstance through God's eyes, with compassion, understanding, mercy, and love.

When I learned this process I said, "Yes, but what if he *is* having an affair?" Let's look at that situation through the lens of this same process.

Event: You just found out that your husband has been having an affair. (This is actually true, not the result of a twisted core belief or an assumption.)

FLESHLY EXAMPLE OF PROCESS	GODLY EXAMPLE OF PROCESS
THOUGHT:	*THOUGHT:*
It's because I've said no too many times.	My husband has a spiritual problem.
He's not attracted to me anymore.	This does not mean that he's not attracted to me or that it's my fault.

FLESHLY EXAMPLE OF PROCESS (CONT'D)	**GODLY EXAMPLE OF PROCESS (CONT'D)**
THOUGHT:	*THOUGHT:*
This is my fault.	We need help from our pastor or a counselor to work through this.
FEELINGS:	*FEELINGS:*
Unforgiveness, anger, hatred, jealousy, bitterness.	Compassion for the spiritual condition that he's in, grief over a broken covenant, disappointment, hope.
RESPONSE:	*RESPONSE:*
File for divorce and "take him for all he's worth."	Discuss the offense and pain involved.
Refuse to let him see the kids.	Seek counsel from a pastor or counselor.
Refuse to forgive him.	Seek God for healing in your heart and start the process of forgiveness.
Slander his name to anyone who will listen.	Share only with those who will wash you in the Word of God for support, comfort, and encouragement.

FLESHLY EXAMPLE OF PROCESS (CONT'D)	GODLY EXAMPLE OF PROCESS (CONT'D)
RESPONSE:	*RESPONSE:*
Cheat on him to get back at him.	Remain true to your God.
Blame yourself.	Look honestly at your own behavior.

You need to know something important: Regardless of the situation, it takes only one person to forgive but two people to reconcile. You may follow this process, taking every thought captive, experiencing healthy emotions, and responding in a godly way yet not experience the outcome that you desire. In the example listed above, the husband's *will* is an important factor. God did not make us robots. He set the biblical standard and commanded all of us to follow it. But we choose whether or not to submit our will to his will. While the Bible permits divorce when there has been adultery, divorce is not God's will. In order for there to be reconciliation, both individuals must be

IT TAKES ONLY

ONE PERSON TO

FORGIVE BUT TWO

PEOPLE TO

RECONCILE.

willing to submit their will to his. Even after we have done so, it still requires a lot of work.

The Bible is all about relationships: A relationship between God's people and himself, between mates and family, between believers and unbelievers. But relationships are difficult because they require a never-ending process of dying to self and submitting to God.

In Scripture we find other examples of both the fleshly process and the godly process, beginning with Satan, who was originally a perfect, anointed cherub. (See Ezek. 28:12–13.) He gazed upon God's glory, desired to be like him, attempted to take what he wanted, and became the Enemy of God.

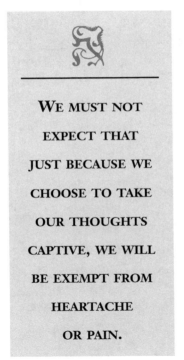

WE MUST NOT EXPECT THAT JUST BECAUSE WE CHOOSE TO TAKE OUR THOUGHTS CAPTIVE, WE WILL BE EXEMPT FROM HEARTACHE OR PAIN.

Eve was the perfect creation of God but was enticed by forbidden fruit and her desire to be like God. She took the fruit for herself and gave it to Adam, ushering sin into the world and earning expulsion from the garden of Eden.

David, the second king of Israel, fell spiritually when he saw Bathsheba and desired her for himself, even though she was the wife of another man. David took her for himself, lied and created a web of deception, and caused the death of Bathsheba's husband, Uriah. The result was a break in David's fellowship with God, the death of his son, and a legacy of sorrow in his family line.

There is something else that we must consider: We must not expect that just because we choose to take our thoughts captive, we will be exempt from heartache or pain. If our spouses break faith with us, whether by adultery or other means, we will experience the agony of a broken covenant. However, by continually taking our thoughts captive, we will, with the help of the Holy Spirit, be able to hold our emotions in check. Then we will be able to go to our knees in prayer and fight the battle that is at hand. (Chapter 12 of this book offers a look at the spirit realm as it pertains to addressing the sins of another person when his actions directly affect us.)

There are other spiritual techniques that we can use to battle against the principalities and spiritual forces that attack our spouses, children, and other loved ones. First and foremost, however, we must understand that we can do everything perfectly and still not see the outcome that we desire. This is due to the fact that, in spiritual battle, someone else's will is often involved.

Donning Our Armor

Prepare your shields, both large and small, and march
out for battle! Harness the horses, mount the steeds!
Take your positions with helmets on! Polish your
spears, put on your armor!

—Jeremiah 46:3–4

*W*hen you became a daughter of the King, you
not only inherited your Father's blessings, but his enemies as well. Knowing this, your Father gave you the
gift of his armor "to stand against the wiles of the
devil" (Eph. 6:11 NKJV). Each piece is distinctive and
unique within itself, but the Princess Warrior must put
on every piece if she is to overcome the attacks of
Satan.

In reading through chapter 6 of Ephesians we can
almost hear the war trumpet sound as the apostle

Paul begins to speak. He tells us to put on armor so that we can be strong against the Devil's schemes. In the Greek, *scheme* means "method." Satan has a PhD in the methodology of spiritual attack. Although it often seems as if his attacks are personal, Satan's larger plan is to disrupt the entire body of Christ. You and I are just one small segment of an entire unit that is under attack. Satan hates everyone who resembles Christ.

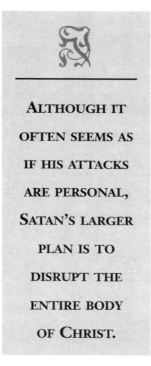

ALTHOUGH IT OFTEN SEEMS AS IF HIS ATTACKS ARE PERSONAL, SATAN'S LARGER PLAN IS TO DISRUPT THE ENTIRE BODY OF CHRIST.

In Ephesians 6 the apostle Paul writes about the outward demonstration of a believer's inward growth and edification. Consider verses 10–20:

Finally, be strong in the Lord and in his
mighty power. Put on the full armor of God
so that you can take your stand against the
devil's schemes. For our struggle is not against
flesh and blood, but against the rulers,
against the authorities, against the powers
of this dark world and against the spiritual
forces of evil in the heavenly realms.
Therefore put on the full armor of God, so
that when the day of evil comes, you may be

able to stand your ground, and after you
have done everything, to stand.

Stand firm then, with the belt of truth
buckled around your waist, with the breastplate of righteousness in place, and with your
feet fitted with the readiness that comes from
the gospel of peace. In addition to all this,
take up the shield of faith, with which you
can extinguish all the flaming arrows of the
evil one.

Take the helmet of salvation and the
sword of the Spirit, which is the word of
God. And pray in the Spirit on all occasions
with all kinds of prayers and requests. With
this in mind, be alert and always keep on
praying for all the saints.

Pray also for me, that whenever I open
my mouth, words may be given me so that I
will fearlessly make known the mystery of
the gospel, for which I am an ambassador in
chains. Pray that I may declare it fearlessly,
as I should.

Paul tells us to "be strong in the Lord and in his
mighty power" (v. 10). The Princess Warrior draws all
the resources that she needs from Christ and his
mighty power. The Greek word for Christ's power here
is *kratos*, the same word for the power that raised Jesus
from the dead and the same power that brought us to
life in Christ when we were dead in trespasses and
sins. It means "to take hold of, grasp, to have power
over, to hold in one's hand." It is a proclamation that

we are not alone, that Christ is not only with us, but that we have the power of Christ at hand. We can, therefore, be strong in his power, knowing that we do not fight the battle alone.

THE ARMOR THAT ASSURES VICTORY

Paul also told us to "put on the full armor of God so that [we] can take [our] stand against the devil's schemes" (v. 11). One of the most wonderful things about our spiritual armor is that the Bible describes God wearing the very same armaments. Isaiah 11:5 tells us that righteousness is God's belt and faithfulness is the sash around his waist. Isaiah 59:17 tells us that righteousness is also his breastplate, that he wears the helmet of salvation on his head, and that he wears the garments of vengeance and wraps himself in zeal as his cloak. What an honor it is to dress ourselves in armor similar of that of our Commander! Our Father knew that every part of our bodies, from head to foot, must be protected, so he created various pieces of armor for our use.

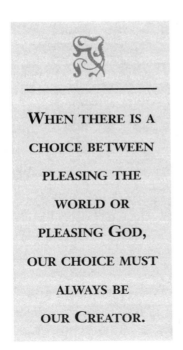

WHEN THERE IS A CHOICE BETWEEN PLEASING THE WORLD OR PLEASING GOD, OUR CHOICE MUST ALWAYS BE OUR CREATOR.

The items of the Princess Warrior's armor appear in the order in which they should be put on as she prepares for battle. Once the armor is on, it leaves no place on her body uncovered.

First, we are to gird our waists with truth. (See Eph. 6:14.) "Truth" in this verse represents both the truth of the Gospel and the truth within us. In biblical battles the belt was crucial because it kept the breastplate in place. Additionally, the sword hung from the belt and needed to be held securely in the same location for easy retrieval. When the warrior wore his belt, it indicated that he was prepared to see action. He loosened it only when he was off duty.

The waist or abdominal area represents the seat of emotions. To gird this area with truth is to commit your emotions to believing the truth. Daughters of the King must hold a commitment to truth regardless of the repercussions. Standing for truth often hurts other people's feelings. That can sometimes be heart-wrenching, but when there is a choice between pleasing the world or pleasing God, our choice must always be our Creator.

Second, we are to put on the breastplate of righteousness. (See Eph. 6:14.) The breastplate covered a soldier's body from the neck to the thighs and covered both the front and back of the solider. "Righteousness" represents integrity of character.

When the Princess Warrior wears the breastplate of righteousness, she deals fairly with others because she is using a biblical standard. She lives life above-board; her actions match her words. She is a woman of character—one who deals honestly, using justice and knowledge.

Once the breastplate has been fitted into position, the Princess Warrior must ready her feet with the gospel of peace. (See Eph. 6:15.) In biblical history, preparing one's feet for war was vital because the terrain one would encounter was often uncertain. It was the one piece of armor that a soldier could not go without, because if his feet were not shod he was limited in his mobility and stability.

THE FIERY DARTS OF THE WICKED ONE ARE OFTEN DOUBT, FEAR, SHAME, GUILT, AND LEGALISM.

The military success of Alexander the Great is said to be, in large part, the result of his army being well shod and able to make long marches at incredible speed over rough terrain. In the same way, when the believer is about her Father's business, ready to go any place to spread the gospel of peace and reconciliation, she needs to prepare her feet for the journey.

In addition, the Princess Warrior is to "take up the shield of faith" (Eph. 6:16). The shield of the Roman solider was generally large and oblong. It consisted of two layers of wood glued together, covered with linen and hide, which was saturated with water, and bound with iron. A soldier's shield provided excellent protection, especially when he fought side-by-side with his fellow soldiers, presenting to the enemy a solid wall of shields.

For the Princess Warrior this protective shield is faith. Remember that faith = trust + belief. When we believe what God's Word says and trust what he says to be true, we can step out in faith against all the fiery darts that the Enemy shoots our way.

In ancient warfare arrows or darts were often dipped in pitch and then ignited to serve as deadly incendiary weapons. The Princess Warrior's shield of faith does not simply deflect such missiles, but it actually quenches the flames to prevent them from spreading. The fiery darts of the Wicked One are often doubt, fear, shame, guilt, and legalism, but the God of Truth enables us to stand and deflect them.

Two more items remain: the helmet of salvation and the sword of the Spirit. The soldier's helmet covered his head and was most commonly made of bronze, with leather attachments.

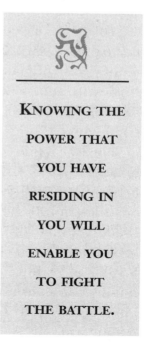

KNOWING THE POWER THAT YOU HAVE RESIDING IN YOU WILL ENABLE YOU TO FIGHT THE BATTLE.

Putting on the helmet of salvation protects the head (see Eph. 6:17), of course, and in the spiritual sense, the mind. When our heads are not covered, any number of thoughts can assault our minds and lead us off course. I have seen many casualties of war in this area when it comes to the assurance of salvation. The Devil puts doubt and insecurity into the minds of believers, and because their heads are not covered with the helmet of salvation, they begin to doubt the side to which they belong. This is what we call brainwashing in today's battles. If the enemy can get into the soldier's head and reprogram his thought process, he can cause devastation.

The last piece of armor that we are told to put on is the sword of the Spirit, which is the Word of God. (See Eph. 6:17.) It is the only offensive weapon in the armor. Luke 4 tells us that when Jesus was combating Satan, he refuted the Father of Lies with the truth of God's Word.

The Word of God is powerful, effective, and instructive (see Heb. 4:12; 2 Tim. 3:16–17), and razor sharp. It is not *your* sword but the sword of the Spirit of God that resides in you. Knowing the power that you have residing in you will enable you to fight the battle at hand with confidence, strength, and surety.

Finally, we are told to pray always. (See Eph. 6:18.) Prayer opens the channels of communication between us and God. In the midst of battle, we as believers must stay in constant contact with our Leader for directions and encouragement. Our prayers for one another are important and effective (see James 5:16), and we must never believe the lie that God does not hear and answer our prayers.

When we pray God makes us alert to what is happening around us. When we pray the Spirit of God teaches us, leads us, and reveals to us the strategies of the Enemy. Many people have difficulty praying because they have failed to put on the armor first. Our flesh doesn't want to pray. Neither does the Enemy want you to pray, because he understands the power that is available to us by calling on the God of creation.

Without the righteousness of Christ, the truth, the gospel of peace, the shield of faith, the helmet of salvation, and the sword of the Spirit, we are not motivated to pray; we want to fulfill the desires of the flesh. In this state, we become vulnerable to the Enemy's taunting, and we become more susceptible to sin.

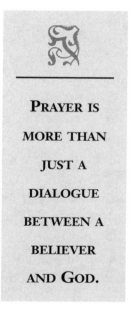

PRAYER IS MORE THAN JUST A DIALOGUE BETWEEN A BELIEVER AND GOD.

THE AGE-OLD TACTIC

Satan's war tactics are subtle but methodical. Like that of many of the historical commanders in armies of the past, Satan's objective is to disrupt communication among the opposing troops. If an army succeeds in interrupting the communication of the opposing commander with his soldiers, that army will win. Believers have a direct line of contact with our Commander twenty-four hours a day, seven days a week. But sin will short-circuit our communication link with God. When this occurs, we must seek the wisdom, forgiveness, and strength of Almighty God. Prayer is more than just a dialogue between a believer and God; it is an avenue that brings intimacy into the relationship and unleashes the power of God himself. It is a place of give and take, where we can learn to be honest and transparent with an all-knowing God, and it is a place to join him in his will.

Scripture tells us to pray without ceasing. Man made prayer a ritual by getting on his knees, folding his palms together, bowing his head, and closing his eyes. Though these practices do promote reverence, consistency, and honor to God, this is not the only way to pray. We can pray to God while standing, with eyes open, with hands raised, whispering, or crying out loud. We can honor him by praying while we are sitting, doing dishes, working on our cars, driving to work, or shopping. He is with us at all times. We should talk to him, praise him, sing to him, thank him, and confess our sins to him. Whatever we do, we should never stop communicating with our heavenly Father.

Hymn writer James Montgomery said, "Prayer is the soul's sincere desire, uttered or unexpressed, the motion of a hidden fire that trembles in the breast."[1] I converse with God about things that I see, feel, or need, and I express my thankfulness for those things that he has given to me or done for me. He fills my thoughts. People are always asking me who I'm talking to—what a great opportunity to witness! Whenever I stop talking to God, I'm confused, lost, and spiritually doomed. I begin to doubt, question, and resist what I know is right. We need him not just some of the time, but all of the time! Jesus is our example, and he prayed for extended amounts of time, especially when making important decisions.

If my husband and I never communicated, we would have no intimacy. We'd be like ships passing in the night. Or what if we spoke only when I wanted something? Or for only a few minutes in the morning, with no communication the rest of the day? What if I did all the talking and never listened to what he had to say? It wouldn't be much of a relationship, would it?

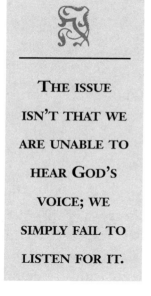

THE ISSUE ISN'T THAT WE ARE UNABLE TO HEAR GOD'S VOICE; WE SIMPLY FAIL TO LISTEN FOR IT.

Conversation with God is critically important in order to maintain a good relationship with him and to retain the power of our Father in warfare. One of the dangers of failing to pray and failing to share our thoughts and feelings is that we tend to nurse grudges toward God because we don't understand why he does what he does. We will not always understand all his reasoning, but in prayer we can come to a place of trust and submission to his will.

When we get caught up in a conflict with God or others, it is often an attack from the Enemy. If we fail to recognize it, we may seek to retaliate in the flesh. But God doesn't want us to respond in that way. We must remember that spiritual attacks require spiritual defense. If we fight in the flesh, everyone loses. If we fight spiritually, our Commander will defend us! If we are in Christ, who can be against us?

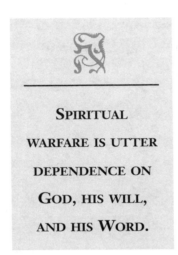

Spiritual warfare is utter dependence on God, his will, and his Word.

One of the most vital aspects of communication is listening. Some people say that they don't "hear" God speak to them. Scripture says, "My sheep listen to my voice" (John 10:27). The issue isn't that we are *unable* to hear God's voice; we simply fail to *listen* for it. Either that or we question it when we hear it because we aren't used to listening!

Prayer is communication with God, a place to claim his promises and to receive his blessings, guidance, and wisdom. One of the greatest things about prayer is that he promises to respond to us, to hear the prayers of the sinner who seeks forgiveness, and to act on the request of everyone who asks in Jesus' name. (See John 14:13–14.) God even answers prayers when we can't find the right words to speak—and he always does more than we ask.

Some say that they don't pray because God already knows their hearts, so why tell him? But it is not enough for God to know our hearts. Do we not want to know his? It is the only way that change will occur in our lives. Prayer is to be an intimate communication between the Creator and his creatures. It would be just as silly for me to say, "Why communicate with my husband when he knows how I feel?" Many believers have needs that go unmet simply because they do not pray. (See James 4:2.)

Prayer is also an expression of dependence upon God. When we go to him with our concerns, we are saying, "I know that I cannot make it through this day and live according to your will without you. I need you. I need your Spirit to guide me." This dependence is at the core of spiritual warfare. In battle we are clinging to nothing more than God. That's it—period. Spiritual warfare is utter dependence on God, his will, and his Word. Our prayers must be in agreement with what God has done in the past, what he is doing at the present, and what he promises to do in the future.

Prayer is our direct line to our Commander. Through prayer God offers direction and encouragement. Furthermore, our prayers are powerful and effective. (See James 5:16.) Consider two biblical characters whom Satan brutally attacked: Job and Nehemiah. Both were attacked—directly and indirectly—by the Enemy, whose purpose was to undermine God's work. Satan often uses other people to attack the believer.

The enemies of Nehemiah ridiculed him, mocked him, and conspired to attack him. And how did Nehemiah respond? By praying in each and every instance of spiritual attack. Numerous times. Nehemiah never took action without first consulting God in prayer.

The same was true of Job. As we read in the book of Job, Satan accused Job before God and robbed him of his health, his wealth, and his children. Job's wife ridiculed him and encouraged him to curse God. His friends unjustly accused him of sin. Job's response? He prayed and praised God, trusting in his Redeemer and proclaiming God's righteousness.

In response to the prayers of both men, God was faithful and blessed them. One of the key ingredients that empowered their prayers was their willing submission to God. Scripture tells us that we must submit ourselves to God and resist the Devil, and then he will flee. We submit to God by being obedient, putting on the full armor as he commands. It is then that we are able to resist the Devil. And when we pray like that to God, Satan will flee. Guaranteed.

IT IS AN HONOR FOR US TO PUT ON THE ARMOR THAT GOD HAS PROVIDED.

Once we cover ourselves with the armor and pray, we are to "stand against" the wiles of the Enemy. The word *stand* is a military term that means "to hold one's position." The armor enables the Princess Warrior to ward off the attacks of the Enemy and to take a stand against him. Before the Princess

Warrior is able to launch any offensive, she must maintain her own ground. The word *stand* is used four times in Ephesians 6:10–18, emphasizing the need for steadfastness in the face of our ruthless foe. The word *against* stresses the determined hostility that is confronting the Princess Warrior. The commander in chief of the opposing forces is the Devil himself. He is a master of ingenious strategies, and we must not allow him to catch us unaware.

THE VALUE OF HEDGES AND ANGELS

In addition to his armor, God provides for the believer two other types of protection. The first is the hedge of God that the Devil complained about in Job 1:10: "Have You not made a hedge around him, around his household, and around all that he has on every side?" (NKJV). This hedge cannot be penetrated without God's permission, and it identifies which side of the battle you are on.

God also provides his angels, who continually minister to believers: "For He shall give His angels charge over you, to keep you in all your ways" (Ps. 91:11 NKJV) and "are they not all ministering spirits sent forth to minister for those who will inherit salvation?" (Heb. 1:14 NKJV).

We are told first to put on the full armor of God, that we may be able to stand firm against the Enemy's attacks. The "hedge" and God's angels are not our only means of protection. Scripture also admonishes us to stand and fight. God not only protects us; he also gives us detailed instructions on how to defend ourselves. He even provides specialized training for us.

History shows us that infantries are often defeated due to a lack of field training. Just as military soldiers become stronger as they continually train, spiritual warriors become stronger in Christ when they continually train in the use of his armaments. Then when war breaks out, they are prepared. Another factor that leads armies into defeat is low morale. We as believers may also develop low morale when we become discouraged, when we lack support from other believers, or when we grapple with inner conflict because we have failed to cover ourselves with the word of God!

It is an honor for us to put on the armor that God has provided. It is our uniform, and it identifies on which side we fight. It says to the Devil, "I am the daughter of *the King*. I am not intimidated by you. I am prepared. My ways are my Father's ways. You are a defeated foe, and because of that knowledge and guarantee I walk in the freedom of faith." The seal of the Holy Spirit is the spiritual covering that signifies four truths: a provision of security, a mark of ownership, a certification of genuineness, and a sign of approval.

Prayer is indispensable to the putting on of God's armor. It enables us to have confidence that the armor will protect us. We can be sure that when we prayerfully and confidently don the equipment that God has provided, we will never experience defeat.

The Power of the Tongue

God's Word that is conceived in your heart, then formed by the tongue, and spoken out of your own mouth, becomes a spiritual force releasing the ability of God within you.

—Charles Capps

The tongue is powerful. Accompanied with faith (belief + trust), it can build up; it also has the power to destroy. Oh, that we could grasp the full understanding of the power of our words! The Bible is not silent on the use of this power.

> Reckless words pierce like a sword, but the tongue of the wise brings healing. (Prov. 12:18)

The tongue that brings healing is a tree of
life, but a deceitful tongue crushes the spirit.
(Prov. 15:4)

He who guards his mouth and his tongue
keeps himself from calamity. (Prov. 21:23)

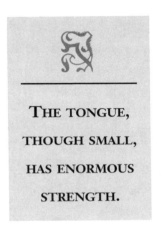

THE TONGUE, THOUGH SMALL, HAS ENORMOUS STRENGTH.

The tongue, though small, has enormous strength. Like a river, the words that flow from the mouth carve out a path. At times that path can be like a gentle and pleasant stream that runs through a backyard. At other times it floods our homes and destroys everything it touches.

Matthew 12:34 tells us that, just as a river has its source, so do our words. They flow from the heart: "For out of the overflow of the heart the mouth speaks." Romans 10:9–10 even tells us, "If you confess with your mouth, 'Jesus is Lord,' and believe in your heart that God raised him from the dead, you will be saved. For it is with your heart that you believe and are justified, and it is with your mouth that you confess and are saved."

What our hearts believe, our mouths speak. That's why it is crucial always to examine our core beliefs to see if they are in agreement with God's Word. Once we do that, we can speak the truth and expect the biblical result to manifest itself.

THE WEIGHT OF A WORD

The power of words was evident even before the earth began. John 1:1 says, "In the beginning was the *Word*, and the *Word* was with God, and the *Word* was God." In Genesis 1 we also read that God spoke: "And God said, 'Let there be light,' and there was light.... And God said, 'Let there be an expanse between the waters to separate water from water,' ... and it was so" (1:3, 6–7). The creation of the world came about through God's spoken word.

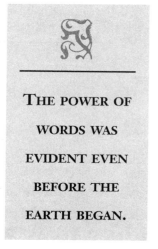

THE POWER OF WORDS WAS EVIDENT EVEN BEFORE THE EARTH BEGAN.

This is an important aspect of spiritual warfare because we tend to defeat ourselves with negative or ungodly talk. Furthermore, some believers become stagnant in their prayer lives because they are not verbally claiming the freedom in Christ that is theirs. This is not some name-it-and-claim-it theology. Rather, it is to believe what God's Word says is true and then to speak it, just as Romans 10:9–10 says to do. This type of verbal faith in action has the power to lead us to salvation and to empower us to overcome trials, resist temptations, and tear down strongholds. It also produces fruit in the lives of other people.

Sarah (not her real name) was going through great difficulty in her marriage. Her husband, Bill, had been trapped in the web of pornography for many years. To make matters worse, he was at times verbally and physically abusive to her. She wanted to storm the gates of hell so that her marriage would survive, but

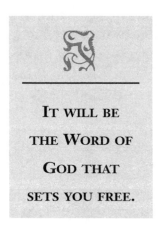

It will be the Word of God that sets you free.

she found herself immobilized by her pain. In her spiritually weak state she would pray, "Lord, I pray that if it's your will, my marriage will survive this difficulty. Please deliver my husband from his addiction to pornography and anger. In Jesus' name, Amen."

Is there anything wrong with that prayer? Yes. There is defeat written all over it. It is covered with doubt and disbelief. Is it God's will to save her marriage? Absolutely. Is it God's will to free her husband from pornography and from the anger that is manifesting itself in his abusive behavior? Certainly. It *is* God's will that Sarah's marriage survive, that she not live in fear, and that her husband be freed from his addictions. A more powerful prayer involves faith (belief + trust) that what God's Word says is true:

> Lord, your Word says that you honor marriage
> and want the marriage bed to be kept pure.
> You have said that you hate divorce and that
> Jesus came to set the captives free. My hus-
> band has been held captive by lust and anger,

and I pray that he would accept the freedom that you offer him in the name of Jesus. You also say in Jonah 3:8 that it's your will that man give up his evil ways and his violence. Lord, I know that it's your will that my husband be delivered from this, so I pray that he will miraculously align his will with yours. It was you who softened the

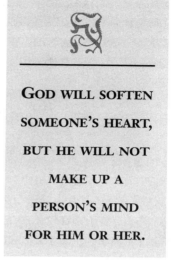

GOD WILL SOFTEN SOMEONE'S HEART, BUT HE WILL NOT MAKE UP A PERSON'S MIND FOR HIM OR HER.

heart of the pharaoh, allowing Moses and your people to walk away in freedom. I accept that same blessing in my marriage. It is in the power that raised Jesus Christ from the dead that I pray. Amen.

That prayer is one of power because it is from the Word of God, and it was the Word of God that brought the universe into existence. It was the Word of God that raised Jesus from the dead, and it will be the Word of God that sets you free from the strongholds and attacks of the Enemy.

Sarah began to pray, believing that God would do the work that he spoke of in his Word. As she began to pray in faith, Bill's heart softened. He began attending a men's group that helps sex addicts. He also took an anger management class and learned to express his feelings and his anger in godly ways. Bill and Sarah have reconciled and today are involved together in fruitful ministry helping other couples.

God's Will and Our Will

Another issue is the will: God's will, our will, and the will of others with whom we come in contact. Knowing God's will and following it requires prayer and a commitment to studying and obeying his Word. But there is a factor other than our will that comes into play. Even if we know God's will and are walking in it, we must also consider the will of others who are involved.

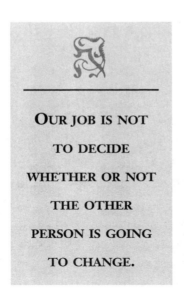

Our job is not to decide whether or not the other person is going to change.

God did not make us robots; instead, he gave us free will. We make our own choices, making decisions and living with their consequences. The decisions of other people also affect us. Vast numbers of people are in counseling because of sexual and physical abuse, a mate's pornography problem, or their parents' alcoholism. God will soften someone's heart, but he will not make up a person's mind for her. The choices are hers and hers alone.

There are many women who have prayed the same powerful prayer as Sarah did, but their husbands did not change. Instead, the husbands went further into sin. Some of them never returned. Is that because the women didn't pray hard enough or long enough? No. It is because their mate's will never aligned with God's. Our job is not to decide whether or not the other person is going to change. Our responsibility is to pray God's Word and to rely on him to lead us in our prayers. If we are seeking God's will, he will reveal to us every step to take and when to take it.

As we pray God's will, the "faith factor" is crucial. We must believe that what we are saying is true. If we don't believe, we need to confess it to the Lord as sin and ask him to build the faith in our hearts and cover ourselves with his Word.

Artist Nicol Smith was one of the first Christians I met after receiving Christ as my Savior. Although she was not yet a famous performer, God's anointing on her and her ability to enter his presence through worship was just as powerful. Her example of how to enter into the presence of God spoke volumes to me in my immature state. One day as we sang together, preparing to minister in a prison, we were singing the hymn "It Is Well with My Soul." In the middle of the song, Nicol stopped and looked me straight in the eye. In a tender voice she said, "You know, Leslie, it's just as easy to sing a lie as it is to tell a lie. The key to worship is being honest before God—aligning your heart with your words." I've never forgotten that piece of wisdom, and every time I am in worship I ask myself if I really mean what I'm saying or if I'm just giving the Lord lip service.

THE AUTHORITATIVE WORD

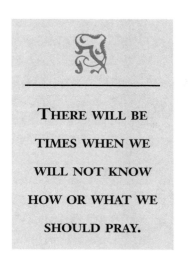

THERE WILL BE TIMES WHEN WE WILL NOT KNOW HOW OR WHAT WE SHOULD PRAY.

In October of 2002 I received an invitation to the White House to attend the Missing, Exploited, and Runaway Children's Conference hosted by President George W. Bush and First Lady Laura Bush. I had the pleasure of meeting the President and talking with him briefly about his faith in God. I will never forget the words that this godly man spoke. When he speaks, he does so with great power and authority. When President Bush gives orders, those who are under his command carry out his wishes without hesitation. But as much power as the President's words have, their power is nothing in comparison to the power of God's words in the lives of those who trust and live by those words.

To what degree are God's words authoritative in our lives? When God says something, do we question it, or do we walk in it without hesitation? Do we bathe ourselves in the truths that he's spoken, or do we dismiss them? We ought always to claim God's words as truth, speak them out, and walk obediently in them.

Knowledge of the power of God's Word is vital for the Princess Warrior because it is his Word that enables us to walk in freedom. There are promises in God's Word for the woman who calls out to him, and his promise is deliverance: "In the day of my trouble I will call upon You, for You will answer me" (Ps. 86:7 NKJV). "Call to Me, and I will answer you, and show you great and mighty things, which you do not know" (Jer. 33:3 NKJV).

There will be times when we will not know how or what we should pray. At such a time, it is sufficient to come into his presence on our faces, weeping and confused, knowing that Jesus is at the right hand of God interceding for us. Our words have the power to heal or destroy. God's Word, when we obey it, live by it, and speak it out boldly, has the power to defeat every foe. Our words, when they are God's words, are powerful indeed. And when we speak them in the power and conviction of the Holy Spirit, relying on him, we are invincible.

The Holy Spirit's Role in Spiritual Warfare

But I say, walk by the Spirit, and you will not
carry out the desire of the flesh.

—Galatians 5:16 (NASB)

J am excited. If you comprehend the power of the Holy Spirit, you will learn everything that you need to know as he leads and guides you in your walk with Christ, as well as in the battles that will follow. Without the Holy Spirit there could be no victory. It is the Holy Spirit who goes before us and enables us to do all things through Christ who strengthens us.

The Holy Spirit is the Princess Warrior's most reliable source of help in both her defensive and offensive strategies. Apart from him, she has no hope for success on the battlefield. He provides direction, wisdom, truth, clarity, strength, and knowledge even of the underlying motives of the Enemy.

OUR HELPER AND OUR BREATH

Jesus called the Holy Spirit the "Helper," which refers to "one who is called alongside" another. Like God the

GOD NEVER INTENDED US TO PLACE HIS HOLY SPIRIT IN A SPIRITUAL BOX.

Father and God the Son, the Holy Spirit is omniscient, omnipresent, and omnipotent. His role is to create, convict, regenerate, baptize, fill, and empower believers. He indwells, teaches, guides, and intercedes for us. These are the attributes of the one who comes alongside us.

When we rely on him to guide us, we are accessing the power of God! As powerful as he is, however, resist the temptation to picture him as a kind of spirit "Terminator." He is also gentle, patient, joyful, kind, faithful, and self-controlled. What a beautiful contrast! The Spirit of God is the everlasting breath of God. In fact, the word *Spirit* comes from the Greek word *pneuma*, which also means "breath."

Genesis 2:7 tells us that when the Lord formed man from the dust of the ground, he "breathed into his nostrils the breath of life." Likewise, at your birth, after nine months inside your mother's womb, you broke the silence with a strident cry as you took your first breath—a breath that you received from God himself.

We cannot live without the breath of God. We can fast, abstaining from food and drink for days, or deprive ourselves of earthly pleasures, denying our passions, and still live. We cannot, however, live without breath. A person may hold his breath for a while, even to the point of losing consciousness. Even at that point, however, he will begin again to breathe spontaneously.

It is the breath of your Almighty Creator that gives you life and enables the rest of your anatomy to function. You cannot live without it. God is life, and life is in his breath. Therefore, you cannot live without him.

The Holy Spirit has been active in your life ever since the day you were born. When you were an unbeliever, the Holy Spirit courted your soul, revealing your need for something more than your earthly existence, which you found to be so unsatisfying. In response to his wooing, you accepted the gift of salvation and received the gift of the Holy Spirit, or "Helper," to assist you on your journey to intimacy with Christ. (See John 14:16 NASB.)

Many uninformed new believers tend to place the Holy Spirit in a box, opening it for use only on Sunday mornings. In essence, they downgrade him from a member of the Trinity to someone who simply gives believers the "warm fuzzies." As a result, immature believers become dissatisfied and begin to see their conversions as merely emotional experiences and not the supernatural transformations that God promised. God never intended us to place his Holy Spirit—God's very breath—in a spiritual box, going dormant except for occasional use. His role is to be a partner, walking beside us and aiding us in battle.

CONVERSATION WITH HIM

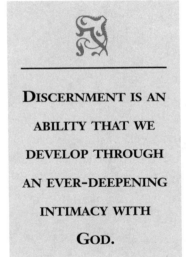

DISCERNMENT IS AN ABILITY THAT WE DEVELOP THROUGH AN EVER-DEEPENING INTIMACY WITH GOD.

When the Bible tells us to pray without ceasing (see 1 Thess. 5:17 NKJV), it is not an unattainable challenge meant to discourage us; rather, it is an encouragement for us to continue walking in the Spirit and engaging in ongoing conversation. It is not difficult to pray without ceasing. We naturally engage in conversation with a person who walks with us, don't we? There are times of silence, but only because we are listening. We are continually to bring our conversation under the submission of the Holy Spirit for a check of what claims to be truth. When we converse with him, he uncovers our motives, revealing our options for Christlike living and our need for dependence upon God. It is a relationship of sheer beauty.

When you hear believers talk about "discernment," what they are talking about is revelation from the Holy Spirit. It can come in the form of a picture, a word, or simply a feeling. Few people actually claim to hear God speak to them in an audible voice. It is more frequently a prompting, a silent whisper in the mind, or a strong sensation in the

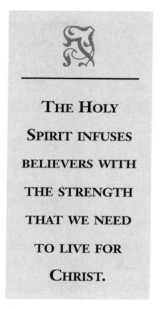

THE HOLY SPIRIT INFUSES BELIEVERS WITH THE STRENGTH THAT WE NEED TO LIVE FOR CHRIST.

soul. Discernment is an ability that we develop through an ever-deepening intimacy with God. The Holy Spirit offers to us the gift of intimacy, which results in the ability to discern. In this intimate relationship, we build trust, becoming sure of God's promises and living out our faith.

When Jesus was leaving his earthly life, he gave the Holy Spirit to believers as a gift for us to have throughout our lives. He said,

> It is to your advantage that I go away; for if I do not go away, the Helper will not come to you; but if I depart, I will send Him to you.... When He, the Spirit of truth, has come, He will guide you into all truth; for He will not

speak on His own authority, but whatever He
hears He will speak; and He will tell you
things to come. He will glorify Me, for He will
take of what is Mine and declare it to you. All
things that the Father has are Mine. Therefore
I said that He will take of Mine and declare it
to you. (John 16:7, 13–15 NKJV)

Like sour milk [sin] curdles in our spirits and we long to rid our spirits of it.

Jesus promised his disciples that, although he was leaving this world, he would never abandon them. He would always be with them in the person of the Holy Spirit, who is equal to both God the Father and God the Son. The Holy Spirit infuses believers with the strength that we need to live for Christ in the midst of daily battles and the ability to bear the fruit of Christian virtues. When we receive the gift of the Holy Spirit, we are, in a real sense, also receiving God the Father and God the Son. We have at our disposal a serious arsenal of power.

To Grieve or Not to Grieve

The Holy Spirit dwells in our hearts and empowers us to serve the Lord. Although the Holy Spirit enters our lives to help us live for God, he does not turn us into robots. We constantly battle the sin nature, and at times we fail. When we willfully continue to sin, however, we grieve the Holy Spirit. The believer who walks with the Holy Spirit will immediately recognize this grieving of the Holy Spirit. We then need to recognize that we have sinned, repent of it, accept God's Truth, and turn away from that behavior in the future. But that is not always what we do.

When we grieve the Holy Spirit we often ignore his grieving in our souls. Like a five-year-old child who doesn't want to hear what someone else is saying, we plug our spiritual ears and scream, "I can't hear you!" We may even mask this grieving with alcohol, drugs, spending, or food. The sin in which we have participated seems at the time more rewarding than the freedom that accompanies walking in Christ. Sin is pleasurable for a season. Then, like sour milk it curdles in our spirits and we long to rid our spirits of it.

When we ignore the Holy Spirit, we are ignoring God.

When we come face-to-face with sin, we have a choice: we can nurture it in order to fill a felt need, thereby eventually creating a stronghold for the Enemy. Or we can submit our felt needs to the Holy Spirit, who will fill that need with Truth. The same is often true about illness. Some people choose to

WHEN WE LIVE IN DEPENDENCE ON GOD'S SPIRIT, WE WILL DISCOVER THAT GOD WILL PROVIDE EVERY TOOL THAT WE NEED IN ORDER TO ACCOMPLISH HIS WILL.

remain sick because their need for the attention that they get is far greater than the benefits that accompany health.

To have the Holy Spirit with us and in us is a great privilege. It is also a great responsibility to listen to him and then respond in a godly way. When we ignore the Holy Spirit, we are ignoring God and we are no longer receptive to change. On the other hand, when we welcome the Holy Spirit to lead and guide us, we flourish!

The Holy Spirit is like a compass that guides the Princess Warrior. Let us consider just a few benefits of relying on the Holy Spirit:

- He will guide you. (See Acts 8:29; Rom. 8:14.)
- He will be your teacher. (See John 14:26.)
- He will testify of Jesus. (See John 15:26.)
- He will intercede on your behalf. (See Rom. 8:26.)
- He will counsel you. (See John 14:16.)
- He will sanctify you—that is, set you apart for a special purpose. (See 2 Thess. 2:13.)

- He will convict you. (See John 16:8–11.)
- He will accomplish regeneration (or change) in your life. (See John 3:6.)
- He will make you aware of sin in yourself and others. (See John 16:8.)
- He will guide you into all truth. (See John 16:13.)
- He will convince you of the truth of the gospel. (See John 16:8, 13–14.)
- He will empower you to witness. (See Acts 1:8; 4:31.)
- He will destroy the power of sin in your life. (See Rom. 8:2–6.)
- He will lead and even control your life. (See Rom. 8:14; Gal. 5:16, 25.)
- He will dwell in you. (See John 14:17.)
- He will remind you of what Jesus said. (See John 14:26.)

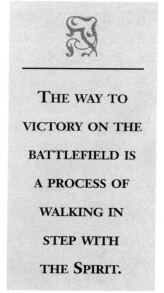

THE WAY TO VICTORY ON THE BATTLEFIELD IS A PROCESS OF WALKING IN STEP WITH THE SPIRIT.

When we live in dependence on God's Spirit, we will discover that God will provide every tool that we need in order to accomplish his will. But let us not fool ourselves. We cannot live the life of a Spirit-filled Christian if we place him in a box, stifling

God's desire to work through him in our lives. The way to victory on the battlefield is a process of walking in step with the Spirit.

The apostle Paul prayed in the first chapter of his letter to the Colossian church a petition that is still applicable today. He prayed that believers would have spiritual wisdom and understanding. The word *spiritual* means "by the assistance of the Holy Spirit." *Wisdom* refers to "skill, tact, aptitude, and expertise in trade." This petition is needed in spiritual warfare as the Princess Warrior accesses the power of heaven that resides within her through the Holy Spirit. My prayer for you is that you will rely on the Holy Spirit, who is eager to assist you. May you walk in step with the Spirit so that you can engage in spiritual battle with great skill.

Satan's Tactics

Your enemy the devil prowls around like a roaring
lion looking for someone to devour.

—1 Peter 5:8

*J*esus said, "When a strong man, fully armed, guards his own house, his possessions are safe. But when someone stronger attacks and overpowers him, he takes away the armor in which the man trusted and divides up the spoils" (Luke 11:21–22). The strong man to whom Jesus referred is us, and the stronger man is Satan.

Satan is the ruler of the world system, a fallen angel, and the ruler of the kingdom of the air. But there is good news: even though Satan's purpose is to destroy God's work, Jesus came to destroy the

IT IS COMMON FOR BELIEVERS TO ASSIGN SATAN MUCH MORE POWER THAN HE ACTUALLY HAS.

works of the Devil. Furthermore, God created Satan, which means that Satan is in no way God's equal. Though Satan is superior to man in intellect and strength, he is inferior to God in every way. Some people say that Satan is the opposite of God, but God has no opposite. Nothing is even remotely comparable to him. It is common for believers to assign Satan much more power than he actually has and to allow that falsehood to intimidate them. While it is true that *apart from Christ* we are all helpless, we have the power *in Christ* to overcome Satan.

SATAN'S OBJECTIVE

One of the keys to success in spiritual battle is understanding the various tactics that Satan uses against us. And we must understand those tactics from the perspective of one of Satan's goals: to strip us of all our armor. In chapter 6 we discussed the armor that God has given us and what each piece represents. Because it covers us from head to toe, Satan wants to steal it from us so that we become vulnerable to direct attack.

Consider again what he desires to steal from us:

- The truth of God's Word (what girds our waists)
- Righteousness (our breastplates)
- The gospel of peace (shoes for our feet)
- Our faith (our shields)
- Our salvation (our helmets)
- The Spirit of God (our swords)
- Our prayer life (our ultimate covering)

We have our weapons, and Satan seeks to neutralize them with devilish tactics. What are the tactics of the Evil One? He uses conflict between believers, gossip, doubt, unbelief, discouragement, and the distortion of the truth.

UNRESOLVED CONFLICT AND GOSSIP

The primary tactic that Satan uses to strip us of our armor is turning believers against other believers. In doing so he can produce mass casualties among the body of Christ, in a sense hitting two birds with one stone. When one believer offends another, the tendency is

THE PRIMARY TACTIC THAT SATAN USES TO STRIP US OF OUR ARMOR IS TURNING BELIEVERS AGAINST OTHER BELIEVERS.

for the believers to become indignant and to assume that their own perspectives are correct. They become consumed with pain and anger and inadvertently loosen their armor, making it easy for the Enemy to slip it off of them. If both believers take this stance, they create a battle within the body of Christ, and they war against their own. Nearly everyone has seen this happen within the church. The truth of God's Word goes out the window, with righteousness on its heel. One or both parties begin slandering and gossiping about the other; soon the church is divided and the Spirit of God is grieved. Each side will pray with his "support group" but will refuse to pray with the other. They pray that the opposing sides will see the truth, which in most cases is according to their own perspectives. All this time Satan sits back in hell, laughing, because with just a little temptation he has produced mass casualties in the body of Christ.

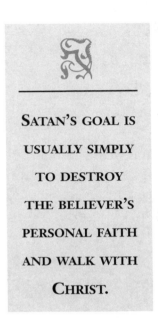

SATAN'S GOAL IS USUALLY SIMPLY TO DESTROY THE BELIEVER'S PERSONAL FAITH AND WALK WITH CHRIST.

While it may be true that Satan has the power to kill a believer—though never without permission from God—Satan's goal is usually simply to destroy the believer's personal faith and walk with Christ. Satan knows that if the believer is dead, he has lost, because Scripture promises that if we are absent from the body, we are present with the Lord. (See 2 Cor. 5:8.) Once our bodies are dead, our spirits are escorted to heaven, where Satan no longer has the power to deceive us. Satan would rather wound us, prompting us to turn our backs on God and other believers. If he can tempt us to gossip or slander those in the church, to lie or steal from the spiritual family, or to hold a grudge, he can use one individual to cause multiple casualties. When one believer sins against another, the offended individual often retaliates. The "victim" begins telling other people about how he was harmed.

WOUNDED BELIEVERS OFTEN ACT LIKE UNBELIEVERS.

Few people can hear of an offense against a friend or family member without picking up the defense on behalf of their loved ones. But every story sounds true until we hear the other side, and we seldom take the time to listen to the other person's perspective. Instead, we tend to engage in the slander without questioning the storyteller at all regarding *her* responsibility in the conflict. We generally fail to hold our loved ones to God's standard of resolving conflict and working toward reconciliation. Our failure serves to perpetuate the cycle of unforgiveness, anger, hatred, and judgment.

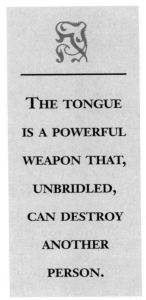

The tongue is a powerful weapon that, unbridled, can destroy another person.

Proverbs 17:9 tells us, "He who covers over an offense promotes love, but whoever repeats the matter separates close friends." That is one of the reasons that gossip and slander are so damaging in the body of Christ. Instead of covering over the offense, we talk about and repeat the matter to others, destroying marriages and friendships. It is tragic to hear on the nightly news how many soldiers we lose daily in a battle in the Middle East. If only we could view the nightly *spiritual* news that God sees, observing the damage that we do to one another. Perhaps it would sound an alarm within us, and beginning with ourselves, believers would become agents of change.

Soon after I became a believer, I began working for a large congregation with a youth pastor and his wife. They had both been emotionally wounded at a previous church and were extremely protective and defensive about their ministry. When God began to work in the lives of the youth group through other leaders, the pastor and his wife became jealous and felt threatened. They gossiped about other leaders until, one by one, the other leaders left the youth ministry. Wounded people hurt others because of their own insecurities and pain. They get caught in the wicked trap of the Enemy, harming themselves as well as causing others to suffer. This couple eventually realized their mistake, asking for forgiveness and seeking to make restitution to the people they had harmed. But the damage they had caused was great. Some left the church, and others even fell away from the Lord.

Wounded believers often act like *unbelievers*—those who have no hope. They get the "it is either them or me" attitude and become pawns in the hands of the Devil. Conflict in the body of Christ is inevitable, but we must be careful not to kill off other parts of our body as we work out our salvation. The Lord gave us very clear instruction in Matthew 18:15–20 regarding how we are to handle disagreements. The process does not include gossip, slander, hatred, or unforgiveness.

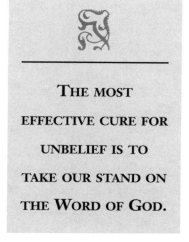

THE MOST EFFECTIVE CURE FOR UNBELIEF IS TO TAKE OUR STAND ON THE WORD OF GOD.

The tongue is a powerful weapon that, unbridled, can destroy another person. "Out of the abundance of the heart [the] mouth speaks" (Luke 6:45 NKJV), revealing either our trust in the Lord or our lack of faith. Why would unbelievers ever consider committing their lives to a God when his followers are in constant conflict with one another? We must set the example of hope in Christ if we expect others to embrace the Savior. Unresolved conflict is one of Satan's chief tactics for neutralizing us in spiritual battle. Another favorite battle tactic of the Evil One is stirring up doubt and unbelief.

DOUBT AND UNBELIEF

Other tactics that Satan employs to attack believers are doubt and unbelief. Satan said to Jesus, "If you are the Son of God ... " (Matt. 4:3) even though he knew full well that Jesus was the Son of God. He used the word *if* in an attempt to create doubt in our Savior's mind. *If* is a big word that Satan often uses.

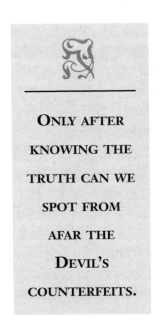

ONLY AFTER KNOWING THE TRUTH CAN WE SPOT FROM AFAR THE DEVIL'S COUNTERFEITS.

Through this small word, he breeds doubt in the heart of the believer. "If you are the daughter of God, then why do you keep failing?" or "Did God *really* say ...?" We must learn to bring every thought to Christ and combat unbelief with God's Word, just as Jesus did. "The Word of God says ..." is a powerful weapon, but we can't use it if we don't know God's Word. Remember the cognitive or mental process that we discussed in chapter 5? We are to compare our thoughts to what God's Word says. The most effective cure for unbelief is to take our stand on the Word of God. When the first two tactics of the Devil fail, he will often turn to his old standard: discouragement and distortion.

Discouragement and Distortion

Satan loves to discourage us. He will use circumstances, people, and our pasts. Discouragement is one of his most effective tools. When we fall prey to this tactic, believing the Devil's accusations and suggestions that we are utter failures, we end up feeling empty. This sense of emptiness will render us ineffective for Christ by making us feel hopeless, weak, and unable to fight. It saps us of initiative. But Christ said that we have the power to overcome through him. He is always ready and waiting for us to return to him so that he may strengthen us by his Word.

Satan also loves to twist God's truth. How can we defend against such a tactic? In banks, new tellers are trained to spot counterfeit hundred dollar bills by first closely examining real ones. They touch, feel, and learn to recognize the genuine currency so that when a counterfeit comes along they are able to spot it immediately. In the same respect, training for spiritual warfare focuses not primarily on the Devil and his methods, but on the genuine power and promises of Christ. Only after knowing the truth can we spot from afar the Devil's counterfeits.

Satan encourages conflict and gossip. He sows

seeds of doubt and unbelief. He discourages believers and distorts the truth. In actuality, the tactics of the Enemy are endless. We will become aware of each of them by knowing God's Word, which will expose Satan's lies. But knowledge of the Devil's schemes is not enough to ensure victory. We must determine in our hearts never to give up. We must push through the furthest limits of our opposition.

Pushing Through the Opposition

The art of war is of vital importance ...
It is a matter of life or death,
a road to either safety or ruin.
—Sun Tzu

*W*hen I was pregnant with my oldest child, I couldn't wait to give birth and experience this new life. The doctors induced labor a month past my due date. I was excited and eager to see the child I'd been carrying for over nine months. They administered a drug called pitocin. Once it entered my body and I experienced my first contraction, I wasn't so excited about induced labor. Hours later, with contractions a minute apart, I was willing to be pregnant for the rest of my life if only the pain would subside. It seemed like forever before the doctors

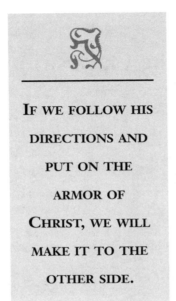

IF WE FOLLOW HIS DIRECTIONS AND PUT ON THE ARMOR OF CHRIST, WE WILL MAKE IT TO THE OTHER SIDE.

allowed me to push and my beautiful daughter was born. Naturally, the pain I'd experienced was eventually overshadowed by the beauty of my child and the experience of being a first-time mom.

When my second child was ready to make an appearance, I was a bit more prepared. The pain was still intense, but I knew that it would end. I knew that I'd overcome the difficulty of labor and that the reward on the other side would be worth every second of the pain.

Such is the case with spiritual battle. When we're in the middle of it, it seems as if it will never end. The ordeal can be excruciating, and doubt assails our hearts, minds, and spirits. But we must not give up. We must believe and trust in God's Word that, if we follow his directions and put on the armor of Christ, we will make it to the other side. We will be stronger and closer to him because of it.

Spiritual battle offers unique challenges through which we must "push." What are the obstacles through which we must overcome? One of the greatest is the baggage that we inherit from the generations that have gone before us. We know that baggage as *generational curses*.

Generational Curses

One reason that we have difficulty pushing through the opposition and overcoming attacks in our lives is because of what we refer to as *generational curses*. They are strongholds that have passed to subsequent generations due to family members' involvement in sin. Another way to regard them is as sinful patterns that have become ingrained in our spiritual blueprints. We all have these curses. They are demonic doorways that others have opened. If we were to draw a "generational chart" of your family tree that displayed your family's strongholds over past generations, it would likely reveal some of the struggles that you or your children may have.

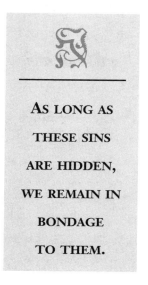

As long as these sins are hidden, we remain in bondage to them.

In my own family tree there is a generational history of sexual addiction, alcoholism, bitterness, self-hatred, and pride. Despite this history I was considered the black sheep of my family, not because I struggled with those same sins, but because I brought them into the open and began a process of healing. How ironic it was that my family accepted me when I walked in the generational curses; once I stepped out of them, however, they rejected me. Satan's goal is for these curses to

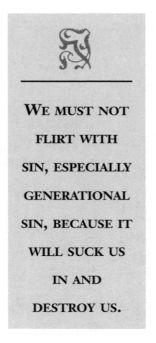

WE MUST NOT FLIRT WITH SIN, ESPECIALLY GENERATIONAL SIN, BECAUSE IT WILL SUCK US IN AND DESTROY US.

remain unaddressed, because as long as these sins are hidden, we remain in bondage to them. My greatest joy is to have served as a pioneer for my mother and brothers, leading the way out of the curses that for generations had bound us.

Why are so many believers subject to generational curses even though they have put their faith in Christ for salvation? How do we overcome generational curses? We begin by understanding some of the mechanics of these curses.

WHY WE STRUGGLE

One reason that we struggle is our tendency to flirt with sin and temptation. When we accept Christ into our hearts, strongholds are broken by the blood of Jesus. But we still have to renounce the strongholds and daily put into practice our freedom in Christ. It takes work, time, dependence upon Christ, and clear boundaries. We must not flirt with sin, especially generational sin, because it will suck us in and destroy us.

The purpose of recognizing our generational curses is to help us become aware of areas of vulnerability. We have all heard people say such things as, "Oh, he's just like his dad. He couldn't stay sober either!" or "She's just like her mother. Money burns a hole in her pocketbook!" It is true that we learn what we are taught, but the truth is even deeper. We are slaves to the curses that we choose *not* to renounce and when we deliberately choose *not* to live in the truth of God's Word.

Another reason that we continue to struggle with certain areas is that we don't really *desire* deliverance. This is because the freedom that comes with deliverance seems less satisfying compared to the sin to which we are enslaved. We are sometimes like the disabled man at the pool of Bethesda, to whom Jesus addressed the question, "Do you *want* to get well?" (John 5:6). We are often satisfied with our dysfunctional manner of life. Throughout most of my childhood I was sexually abused by a neighbor

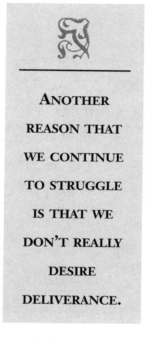

ANOTHER REASON THAT WE CONTINUE TO STRUGGLE IS THAT WE DON'T REALLY DESIRE DELIVERANCE.

and two relatives. Since my father never offered to me appropriate love, I sought love through other means, allowing others to take advantage of me. As uncomfortable and painful as the abuse was, the "love" and "acceptance" that it offered seemed to me a fair trade. I was convinced that if I was to gain love and acceptance, it would have to be through sex. Thus began the cycle of defeat in my life. My behavior heaped shame and guilt upon my young soul. It didn't stop there. I carried that same belief system into my teen years and early adulthood. And because my need for love and acceptance was so intense, I became entrapped in ongoing unhealthy behavior.

THE HOLY SPIRIT IS OUR SAFETY NET WHEN WE LET GO OF A STRONGHOLD AND REACH OUT TO GRASP HOLD OF GOD.

When I became a believer I continued to struggle in this area. It was an unhealthy thought process more than just the act of sex. I continued to engage in casual flirtatious behavior because it fed a deep need in my soul. The attention that men lavished on me confirmed in my mind that I was attractive, loved, and special. When I flirted with someone who did not respond, I saw it as a challenge. My identity became wrapped up in this behavior. I never stood on the corner and prostituted myself for money, but I certainly did so emotionally in order to gain love and acceptance. Interestingly, I didn't actually *enjoy* being promiscuous or flirtatious. I soon identified it as an outward sign of an inward struggle. It was a symptom of a much greater problem: self-hatred, shame, and a failure to grasp my identity in Christ. Those issues had long ago forged chains that needed to be broken, link by link.

BREAKING FREE

I told myself that I *wanted* freedom, but did I? Jesus had already broken the curse, right? Yes, but I still walked around bound by the chains. Grasping freedom meant letting go of the old behavior, the old Leslie, and reaching out to the promise and guarantee of deliverance. But it seemed to me like a "great unknown." I was scared of who I might become or that God would leave me out in the cold. The process of releasing the grip on my stronghold and grasping hold of God's way was similar to the way that a trapeze artist lets go of the bar in order to grasp another. There is a period of time between the two bars when he is in midair, with nothing to hold on to. This is a place of faith, but it can be terrifying. As frightening as it seems, in this truth we can rest assured that we will not fall and hit the ground. It is impossible to fall when we are reaching for Christ. In the popular reality show *Fear Factor*, no matter what stunt a contestant attempts, there is always a safety net in place. The Holy Spirit is our safety net when we let go of a stronghold and reach out to grasp hold of God. Such was the case for me in what I call my "love" addiction that manifested itself through sex.

I slowly began to submit my identity, my needs, and my desires to God. The Holy Spirit prompted me to look for ways to escape flirtatious behavior with men. I avoided eye contact that communicated availability. I shut doors of temptation as soon as they opened. I continually went to God in prayer, saying, "I know that you are there, but I can't see you. Please comfort me." And he did.

GLIMPSES OF VICTORY

In making these changes I began to understand that I was precious to God. A determination emerged: my heart would be given only to the man God had chosen for me. I began to see myself the way God saw me—as a gift to be protected and cherished. It required effort to remain focused on God and not on my insecurities or ungodly desires for attention. I prayed my way through many lonely nights when the Enemy brutally attacked me. My search for freedom was accompanied by many tear-filled nights.

The Enemy of my soul was relentless. I faced attacks at every turn. Men with whom I had flirted in the past suddenly discovered a new, thriving interest in me, sending me flowers, initiating contact. Others flattered me and talked "love" and "romance." It was difficult to resist my old behaviors. I failed many times but never gave up. My goal was total victory.

As I continued to walk in deliverance, I got better at defending my honor in Christ. One day I suddenly sensed that the Lord wanted me to know that he had fully delivered me from my cycle of defeat. The experience of that liberating moment is nearly indescribable. I've walked in deliverance ever since, having learned to rely completely upon him.

FIGHTING THE GOOD FIGHT

To some people the idea of struggling with sexual immorality seems foolish. But we each harbor strongholds and suffer with generational curses. It may be pride, judgment, gossip, alcohol, drugs, spending, or pornography. Maybe you too are in bondage. Every time you try to let go of your demon, temptation slams you. Satan doesn't want you free. He's going to fight to keep you defeated by waving your weaknesses in your face. But keep fighting. Push through and don't give up. Keep pressing for deliverance at the foot of the cross. Freedom will be yours.

Now bear something in mind: One of the greatest tools that Satan will use to keep you in bondage is the approval of other people. I once shared with a Christian friend some unhealthy behavior patterns in which I had formerly participated that hurt other people. I shared with her how God's power had freed me from my behaviors. Sadly, in the midst of relational difficulty that we encountered some time later, she began to attack me by using my past as a weapon. She said things like, "You told me how you used to take advantage of other people, and I'm not going to let you do that to me!" and "You're not trustworthy because of what you've done in your past!"

In the midst of her accusations, the Lord impressed upon me through the prompting of the Holy Spirit that this was a direct assault from the Enemy of my soul. He is the accuser, the one who reminds us of our pasts. He is the one who tells us that we will never change. He is a liar. How should we respond in such a situation? There may be many times when the principles of conflict resolution taught in Matthew 18 will resolve a given situation. However, there may be times when they are not effective or when there is the possibility of physical, emotional, or spiritual harm. Then, we must remove ourselves from the person who is being used by Satan and seek God for divine wisdom for the next step.

There may be times when others will use your past against you, speaking critically of you, even though you may have addressed your issues in a godly manner. Do not allow what others say or do in such circumstances to sway you. Remember who you are in Christ today. Do not permit the fiery darts of the Enemy to penetrate you.

THE USEFULNESS OF STORMS

A few years ago I was traveling alone in a recreational vehicle across the United States. My spiritual journey was at a point where my battles seemed to have no end. In the middle of my trip I encountered a torrential rainstorm. Visibility was nil. To make matters worse, the water flooding the road caused a short circuit in my electrical system, resulting in the loss of my headlights and windshield wipers. I pulled over and stopped, straddling the right shoulder of the interstate highway. Cars and trucks rocketed past, blasting their horns at the huge RV that was taking more than its fair share of the road. I was in imminent danger of a serious accident.

With tears streaming down my face I began to pray for guidance. In his still, small voice God spoke to me. He said, "Leslie, the only way *out* is *through*." I realized at that very moment that he was allowing a rainstorm to teach me a profound spiritual lesson. I didn't want to continue my ongoing spiritual battle any more than I wanted to proceed through that rainstorm.

I continued to cry out to God as I slowly began to move my vehicle forward, turning on my emergency flashers. I drove at a crawl for another forty miles until I reached a truck stop where I was able to get my vehicle repaired (at no cost, I might add). The storm subsided, and I continued to my destination without further problems.

God used that storm in my life to teach me a valuable lesson. He taught me to depend on him in both the physical and the spiritual storms of life. The drive through my storm was difficult. But God was faithful. I had to depend on him every second of the way. Nevertheless, I completed my journey across America. I also survived my spiritual journey—as will you—knowing that the only way *out* is *through* the

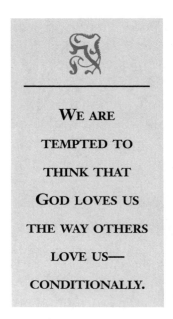

WE ARE TEMPTED TO THINK THAT GOD LOVES US THE WAY OTHERS LOVE US— CONDITIONALLY.

cross of Calvary, depending on the one who sacrificed himself for us on that hill.

LETTING GO OF THE SECRET PLACES

One barrier that I continue to run into as I work out my salvation is the secret compartments in my heart that I do not want to expose, much less push through. I sometimes think that the sin in the crevasse of my heart is too ugly even for God to see, so I conceal it beneath the good things that I do that will please God.

There are parts of us that we don't want to discuss with God. Instead, like Adam and Eve in the garden, we try to hide them from him. What are we afraid of? That he won't love us if we let him see the sin that we are hiding? That it's too big of a sin to be forgiven? We are tempted to think that God loves us the way others love us—conditionally. That is incorrect. When we make God's love conditional we reduce God, humanizing him.

I recall a specific conversation that the Lord and I had one day as I struggled with the sexual promiscuity issue. I didn't want to discuss the issue with him; after all, it was forgiven, wasn't it? Yes, but he wanted to walk through it with me, not to shame me, but to show me the grace, mercy, and love that he had for me. He wanted to show me that who I was in my past is not who I am today. Most of all, he sought to deliver me from the unjustifiable anger that I harbored toward him and the false beliefs I'd held that spurred my need to act out in order to gain love.

Our conversation resembled a tennis match more than a conversation. The Holy Spirit prompted me to read John 11, about the death and the raising of Lazarus. Jesus directed the mourners to take away the stone from Lazarus's tomb. (See John 11:39.) His purpose was to raise Lazarus from the dead and to glorify God.

I came to understand the story as it relates to my sin. God wanted me to uncover that area in my life so that I could experience life and he could be glorified.

"Leslie, take away the stone," I felt him prompt me.

"Uh, I don't think so, Lord," I argued. "You don't understand. I know what's in that white-washed tomb, and it stinks."

"Leslie," he patiently whispered again. "Take away the stone."

In agony I argued, "Are you listening to me, Jesus? It's ugly in there. I can't do it. I'm scared. Besides, what's the point? Don't you think we should leave alone what is decaying?" I knew the biblical answer, but I didn't want to deal with it.

The prompting of the Spirit was gentle but persistent. I read John 11 again.

THE PROBLEM WITH SIN IS THAT IT BREEDS MORE SIN, JUST LIKE ROTTING MEAT BREEDS MAGGOTS.

The story stirred up my own anguish and grief over the experiences of my younger days. My anger toward God poured out. One of my childhood beliefs was that God was hateful and mean because he had allowed sexual abuse to occur in the life of a helpless child. I thought and even told others, "If he really existed, he would have never allowed the abuse to happen."

John 11 opened my eyes to the anger that I was still clutching.

"Where were you, God, when I needed you? How could you just stand idly by while those men stole my innocence?"

As I prayed, I realized that I was verbalizing the same complaint that both Mary and Martha had voiced. "If you would have been here, this would have never happened." (See John 11:21.)

But as I read and reread that passage, the Holy Spirit gently mended my broken heart, soothing the pain from my childhood. I knew at that very moment that God was deeply moved in spirit and was troubled by what had happened to me—that he wept with me. He wept *for me* as that little girl was violated, and he wept *with me* as that young woman began to heal.

When Jesus shed tears of compassion for those who were suffering, the Jews said, "Could not he who opened the eyes of the blind man have kept this man from dying?" (John 11:37). Indeed, he could have. But that would have robbed the Son of God of great glory through the raising of Lazarus. Could he not have stopped my perpetrators from damaging my tender spirit? Yes, but to do so would have stolen away the opportunity for me to share the miracle of restoration in my own life.

Jesus and Martha had played the same type of verbal "tennis" that he and I had over my past. How I can relate to that! When Jesus asked those who were standing by the tomb to move the stone from the grave, Martha argued, as if she was revealing something that the all-knowing God whom she worshipped didn't know: "But Lord ... by this time there is a bad odor, for he has been there four days" (John 11:39).

Sin has an odor. It smells like death—spiritual death—polluting everything around it. Like rank and rotten eggs, its smell instantly nauseates us. It doesn't even have to be our own sin; even the effects of someone else's actions will spark the same reaction. The problem with sin is that it breeds more sin, just like rotting meat breeds maggots. Victims of sexual abuse often become promiscuous and bitter, thereby breeding more sin and, ultimately, more death. The thought of "removing the stone" that covers such ugliness can overwhelm us with revulsion. It is that unpleasant.

THERE IS POWER IN NUMBERS.

Jesus offered Martha profound wisdom when he said, "Did I not tell you that if you believed, you would see the glory of God?" (11:40). This produced in Martha a crisis of belief. Did she believe that God would be glorified if the ugliness of death was exposed? Would he really be able to perform a miracle in this circumstance?

Did Martha hesitate, weighing the options of believing or not believing, before she acted? Or did she instantly respond in faith and remove the stone? Most of us tend to analyze our options before we step out in faith. Martha learned an important lesson when she finally exercised faith. The stone was removed, and Lazarus came walking out in grave clothes. We, like Martha, will see life emerging from death if we are willing to listen, believe, and respond in faith to the Lord.

Losing Our Grave Clothes

Once Lazarus rose from the dead, there remained one more task. Jesus said to those watching, "Take off the grave clothes and let him go" (11:44).

Why was taking off the grave clothes significant? Because they would serve only to bind Lazarus and to surround him with an awful stench. So it is with us. Many wounded people sensationalize their past scars for two reasons. First, when others see our scars, it gives us the opportunity to talk about something that we've overcome. That is good, so long as the goal is to glorify God, telling others how he has enabled us to overcome circumstances. Unfortunately, we often use our testimonies as an opportunity to exalt our own accomplishments and our own strength.

Second, we sometimes believe that if we can continually see the scars in our lives it will remind us not to repeat our past failures. But we don't need the scars from our pasts to assure us of freedom. All we need is Jesus. We can take off the grave clothes that remind us and others of our death and put on the "new coat"—identity in Christ.

THE POWER OF UNITED PRAYER

As you ponder the truths in this chapter, take a concrete action step. Find a confidant who will pray with you and for whom you can pray as you both endure the trials of life. As we cultivate an honest transparency and as we encourage one another with God's Word, it will provide the accountability and strength that we desperately need. Ecclesiastes 4:9–12 tells us that there is power in numbers. When we are in agreement with one another and with the truth of God's Word in prayer, we will see answers that amaze us. Matthew 18:20 further makes this point. "For where two or three are gathered together in my name, there am I in the midst of them" (KJV).

In my prayer ministry, when I gather with several women, we pray about only one subject at a time, with one person praying aloud while the others in the group are praying silently on the same subject. This is a powerful way to pray, tearing down strongholds, claiming territory that was once given over to demonic activity, and empowering the individual to walk in the freedom of Christ.

Assemble four or five women together on a weekly basis. Spend thirty minutes talking about issues in each other's lives. Then spend thirty minutes looking into God's Word to see what he has to say about the subject that the Spirit prompts you to focus on. Finally, gather around each individual, lay hands on her, and speak God's Word over her in prayer while the rest of the group prays silently. The Lord will open your eyes and minister powerfully through you.

PRESS THROUGH, PRINCESS WARRIOR!

When you ponder your battles, think of the garden of Gethsemane. It was a place of sorrow and trouble—overwhelming to the point of death. It was a place of disappointment, betrayal, and deception. Even more so, however, it was a place of prayer, mercy, and a proclamation of God's strength. Jesus pressed through the opposition there and went on to suffer death at the hands of sinful men. But there's another side to that story. He rose again, and because he pressed through the storm we now experience the freedom that comes with his victory. With Jesus as our example we must, in a similar manner, press through whatever we are experiencing. We must know and believe that freedom lies on the other side of the storm.

Spiritual Warfare in Marriage

Therefore a man shall ... be joined to his wife,
and they shall become one flesh.

—Genesis 2:24 NKJV

*T*he most important aspect of spiritual warfare in marriage is the realization that your husband is not the enemy. Regardless of how many issues a couple works through, the core truth that we often lose sight of is that husband and wife are a team, help-mates on the same side of the spiritual battle. Even when our mates sin by saying or doing something offensive, it does not justify an attitude that regards them as the incarnation of Satan. What we need is a new perspective on forgiveness.

A NEW PERSPECTIVE ON FORGIVENESS

There was a season in my marriage when I went through great difficulty. I was struggling to forgive myself for things that I had done in our marriage, as well as to forgive my husband for the things that he'd done. One day as I sat with my friend and Christian

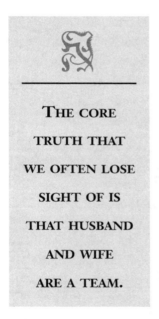

THE CORE TRUTH THAT WE OFTEN LOSE SIGHT OF IS THAT HUSBAND AND WIFE ARE A TEAM.

counselor, Cindy Fitzee, she showed me a picture of Jesus carrying the cross. She said, "Leslie, when you hold yourself to the sins of the past, you are saying that what Jesus did on the cross wasn't enough. In essence, you're saying that you have to carry your own sin, and you're not the Savior of your own life."

It was like she had tossed a lighted match into my soul. Long after I left her office, her words resonated in my spirit. I realized that she was right. I needed to ask for-

giveness from God for trying to carry my own sinful past. What Christ did for me on Calvary was suffi-cient for all my sins—past, present, and future.

After I prayed for forgiveness, the Lord showed me that I was doing the same thing to my husband. If what Christ did on the cross was enough for my sin, it was also enough for his. If what Jesus did on

Calvary could change my life and behavior, it had the power to do the same in my husband's life. Who was I to hold back forgiveness in our marriage? Who was I to be bitter over past offenses?

FORGIVENESS IS NOT AN INVITATION FOR ANOTHER PERSON TO HURT US AGAIN.

I fell to my knees again, this time asking forgiveness for acting as if Christ's finished work on the cross wasn't enough for my husband. Once I prayed that prayer, I was able to view my husband in a whole new light—through the eyes of Jesus.

THE FREEDOM OF FORGIVENESS

Christians make forgiveness much more difficult than it has to be. We want to punish ourselves and others for sins committed. We mistakenly believe that if we forgive someone we are saying that what that person did was OK. Forgiveness is not an invitation for another person to hurt us again; neither does it mean that we will immediately trust that person again.

Forgiveness simply means that we give up our right to hold on to the wrongdoings of others against us. We release them from their debt, accepting the consequence of their actions against us. That's what Christ did. He released us from our debt and accepted a horrific death on our behalf. The truth is that holding a grudge or holding others in debt ensnares *us*, not *them*.

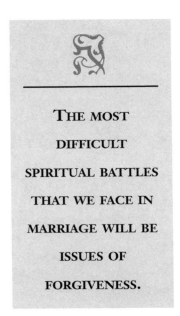

THE MOST DIFFICULT SPIRITUAL BATTLES THAT WE FACE IN MARRIAGE WILL BE ISSUES OF FORGIVENESS.

Accepting the consequences of their actions against us is often simply an issue of perspective. In most cases we are already living with the consequences of the other person's actions. The person who harmed us has usually gone on with his life, unaware of the pain that he has inflicted on us. The most difficult spiritual battles that we face in marriage will be issues of forgiveness. And many of the strongholds with which we struggle—bitterness, hatred, jealousy, gossip, and slander—are the direct result of unforgiveness.

The way to work through the spiritual battle of unforgiveness that rages within us is to keep taking it to the cross and keep giving it over to Jesus. There is a process that I recommend to believers that enables them to break the bonds of a besetting sin— a sin to which they return time and again. I call this process "the Five Rs."

1. **Recognize** that you are refusing to forgive.
2. **Renounce** your sin of unforgiveness.
3. **Rebuke** the spirit of unforgiveness that you've nurtured.
4. **Receive** truth in its place.
5. **Rejoice** in the freedom that you now have in Christ.

Learn and practice these five Rs, and you will discover that forgiveness doesn't make you a victim. It allows you to walk with Jesus as a victorious Princess Warrior. But there are other battles that we must fight. There is another spiritual truth that cuts across the grain for most women in our culture: submission.

IT IS VITAL THAT WE UNDERSTAND THE IMPORTANCE OF BOTH SUBMISSION AND SERVICE IN MARRIAGE.

THE STRUGGLE TO SUBMIT

One of the reasons that we find the topic of submission so distasteful is because we misunderstand its meaning. Another reason is that biblically ignorant people have sought to badger us into an unbiblical form of submission. It is vital that we understand the importance of both submission and service in marriage, or we will live in spiritual defeat in our marriage relationships.

Let's consider a brief biblical history of submission and servanthood:

We all know the story of Adam and Eve in the garden of Eden. God created the world, including the garden of Eden, and he created Adam, placing him in the garden to care for it. It was a paradise, complete with its own river and trees that were pleasing to the eye. God told Adam that he could eat from any tree in the garden, except from the Tree of the Knowledge of Good and Evil. To eat from that tree would result in death.

Then God said, "It is not good for the man to be alone. I will make a helper suitable for him" (Gen. 2:18). And he did. God caused Adam to fall into a deep slumber, and, taking one of Adam's ribs, he created Eve. When Adam awoke and saw Eve he said, "Wow! Holy Moley!" Or something like that. He actually said, "This is now bone of my bones and flesh of my flesh; she shall be called 'woman,' for she was taken out of man" (2:23).

Adam and Eve lived in the garden until the serpent, who was craftier than any of the wild animals that God had made, entered the scene. And where did the serpent head? Where he always goes. He went for the weakest link—something he will always do in our marriages. He went to Eve instead of Adam. He did so for a specific reason.

THE NECK THAT TURNS THE HEAD

There is a saying that goes, "The man may be the head of the family, but the woman is the neck that turns the head." Satan knew that he could get to the man by deceiving the woman. Satan's deception of Eve began with planting a seed of doubt. There was no courteous exchange with the serpent. No "Hey, nice day in paradise, isn't it? How are you today?" No, Satan's first recorded words were, "Did God *really* say, 'You must not eat from any tree in the garden'?" (3:1). Consider your own marriage. What is it that Satan has whispered in your ear? How has he created doubt regarding what God has said about marriage?

I've heard many women apply that same satanic logic to their marriages.

"Did God really say that I must stay married to my husband or never remarry?"

"Did God really say that I have to submit to my husband, even if I don't agree?"

"Did God really say that the only reason I can divorce is because of adultery?"

Back to Eve. She responds by repeating the command that God gave Adam. "We may eat fruit from the trees in the garden, but God did say, 'You must not eat fruit from the tree that is in the middle of the garden, and you must not touch it, or you will die'" (3:2–3). Eve is simply repeating what God said to Adam. In order for her to obey God's directive, she has to believe and trust *who*? Her husband. And to do so, she must be confident that he has advised her correctly.

Satan's response creates doubt and is an obvious contradiction of God's instructions. He says, "You will *not* surely die" (3:4). The snake then slanders God, claiming that he was keeping something good from them: "God knows that when you eat of it your eyes will be opened, and you will be like God, knowing good and evil" (3:5).

Something significant occurred between Satan's final statement and Eve's disobedience. Like all of us, she went through a cognitive or mental process before arriving at a place of rebellion. Let's observe what she experienced as she considered the words of the serpent.

Event: The serpent came to the garden and tempted Eve to partake of the fruit. He told her that God was lying to her and to Adam.

FLESHLY EXAMPLE OF PROCESS	GODLY EXAMPLE OF PROCESS
THOUGHT:	***THOUGHT:***
"What if he's right? I won't die."	"God doesn't lie. I will die."
"The fruit on this tree looks great."	"I need to ask Adam to remind me what God said."
"Did God really say that I can't eat from this tree?"	"This tree is forbidden to Adam and to me."
"Did Adam know what he was talking about?"	"To disobey God will bring judgment."
"God doesn't want me to know the truth."	"I can trust what God says."
FEELINGS:	***FEELINGS:***
Doubt, confusion, desire, mistrust, suspicion.	Confidence, understanding, knowledge, trust.
RESPONSE:	***RESPONSE:***
Partake from the tree.	Walk away from temptation.
Mislead her husband to partake.	Talk with Adam about the encounter with the snake.

Eve made the wrong decision. She not only partook of the fruit, but she gave some to her husband who was with her, and he ate it. Adam failed to restrain or redirect Eve. Ashamed and aware of their nakedness, Adam and Eve hid. God entered the garden and began by calling to them. Adam explained to God that he realized he was naked. God asked Adam if he ate of the forbidden tree. Adam responded by telling the truth, but he shifted the blame first to God for giving Eve to him, then to Eve.

If [Satan] crushes man, he crushes the world.

"The woman you put here with me—she gave me some fruit from the tree, and I ate it" (3:12). Then God spoke to Eve, "What is this you have done?" (3:13). Eve blamed the snake. "The serpent deceived me, and I ate" (3:13). It is true that the snake deceived Eve, but she *chose* to disobey God by believing the lie of the serpent.

God cursed the snake first, saying, "Because you have done this, cursed are you above all the livestock and all the wild animals! You will crawl on your belly and you will eat dust all the days of your life" (3:14). Then God spoke the important conclusion to the curse on the snake. God said in verse 15, "I will put enmity between you and the woman, and between your offspring and hers; he will crush your head, and you will strike his heel." Notice that God first said that there would be enmity—hostility—between Satan and the woman.

A Curse and a Promise

The Hebrew word for "enmity" is *'eybah*, meaning "hatred, hostility; to be an enemy." Satan is your enemy and you are his. God gave women extraordinary power through persuasion, beauty, gentleness, and servanthood. Satan knows that if the same persuasion that he used to lead Adam astray is used for God's glory, he's in bad shape. That is why he is determined to destroy woman and her godly characteristics; if he can do so, he crushes man. If he crushes man, he crushes the world. We do not have far to look in Scripture to see examples of this, from Solomon's wives who led him astray and into worshipping foreign gods to Delilah and her seduction of Samson to Jezebel who walked all over her husband and led his kingdom to ruin.

After cursing the snake, God addressed Eve. He said, "I will greatly increase your pains in childbearing; with pain you will give birth to children. Your desire will be for your husband, and he will rule over you" (3:16). In those moments of greatest blessing—marriage and the birth of children—the woman would sense most clearly the painful consequences of her rebellion against God. Thankfully, along with this discouraging pronouncement there is also a promise: the final victory will belong to the "seed of the woman." In the birth of every child, therefore, there is a reminder of the hope that lay in God's promise. Birth pains are not merely a reminder of the futility of the fall; they are a sign of impending joy as well.

The second part of verse 16 is vital for us to grasp: "Your desire will be for your husband, and he will rule over you." The word *desire* means "to yearn, or long for something that is not yours to possess." As a result, a woman's tendency is to resist her husband's leadership, regarding it as something that *she* should acquire. We don't have to look far in history to see the fulfillment of this judgment. Ever since the fall, woman has been resisting man's leadership, and that is one of the central problems in marriages today.

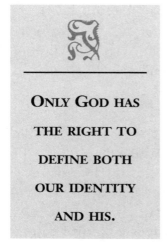

ONLY GOD HAS THE RIGHT TO DEFINE BOTH OUR IDENTITY AND HIS.

This has nothing to do with the essential equality of men and women. It is simply a question of the God-given roles of men and women and the tendency of women to usurp men's roles. It is an issue that women need to address honestly in the body of Christ. And wherever we violate God's plan, we need to repent.

Feminism and Biblical Womanhood

Feminism is a term that means different things to different people. Some who call themselves feminists are interested only in promoting and protecting the biblical dignity and worth of women. Some feminists address valid concerns: the abuse of women, the degradation of women through pornography, and the falsehood that women are of lesser value than men. Others encourage women to decide—apart from the Bible—who they are, what the world should be like, and who God is. But only God has the right to define both our identity and his. When God made the earth, he created man and woman, and he alone determines who they are and how they should live. (See Rom. 9:20–21.)

Scripture tells us that women are made in the image of God. We therefore merit the same dignity and respect as men. But the Bible also describes some basic differences between men and women—differences that we are to honor as part of God's design. (See 1 Cor. 11:3–16.) While the Bible does not promote the degradation or abuse of women, neither does it support the right of women to put themselves above God's plan and do as they please.

The feminist movement began with a group of women who were advocating for the dignity and respect of women as well as their right to an education, to vote, to sign legal documents, and to own their own land. But women, like Eve, were not content with the freedoms that they had won. Power and

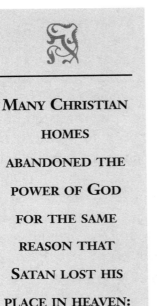

Many Christian homes abandoned the power of God for the same reason that Satan lost his place in heaven: the prideful quest for power.

control is addictive, and women soon began seeking to diminish the authority of men. One of the first recorded documents of the women's rights movement had as its title *Women of the World Unite: We Have Nothing to Lose but Our Men!*[1]

But radical feminism cannot succeed in its attack on the concept of male leadership without attacking the Bible, the family, the church, the sanctity of marriage, and the law. When we try to usurp the role of man, we are seeking the destruction of the plan that God put into place at the dawn of creation. Women were not satisfied merely to gain the right to vote and an education. They became even more aggressive in their attacks on masculine dominance. The earlier women's movements became more radical over time and sought to "expose the white male power structure in all its hypocrisy" in its attempt to give women the freedom to acquire that same power.[2]

During the American Civil War, the women's rights movement very nearly tore the country apart. The radical feminists of this nation accused Judeo-Christianity of being the number one cause of women's suffering. Their incessant propaganda campaigns promoted the idea that the Bible espoused the inferiority of women. Sadly, what the radical feminists regarded as enslavement and inferiority was in actuality freedom, honor, and respect for the role of womanhood. In their relentless search for power, the feminists abandoned the unique role of a woman, leaving the family unit in shambles, marriages broken, and the body of Christ divided.

First Corinthians 1:18 warns us that "the message of the cross is foolishness to those who are perishing, but to us who are being saved it is the power of God." Many Christian homes abandoned the power of God for the same reason that Satan lost his place in heaven: the prideful quest for power. Just like Satan, the radical women's movement has relinquished the most precious possessions that God entrusted to women.

Radical feminists came together in the 1970s and formed consciousness-raising groups with the idea of exploring common themes about the role of women in society. These groups encouraged women to emulate the hierarchical, male-dominated business world and told them that in doing so they would become stronger and more powerful. Some of their meetings would begin and end with ceremonies gleaned from Native American or other ancient pagan cultures. They would bring items that represented power and masculinity and place them at an altar that represented the purging of their feminine role and a seizing

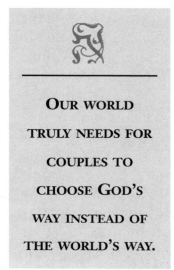

OUR WORLD TRULY NEEDS FOR COUPLES TO CHOOSE GOD'S WAY INSTEAD OF THE WORLD'S WAY.

of the male role. Women were encouraged at this altar to bury the sadness that they associated with their femininity and to move forward in the "power" of masculinity.

Many women followed these groups as they fought for sexual freedom, saying that there was a sexual double standard for men. They struggled for the freedom to engage in sexual promiscuity and to practice lesbianism. They struggled for financial freedom apart from men and for the sole power to run the home and business. They battled for the right to work outside the home and in the process attempted to degrade women who held onto traditional women's roles. One leader from the founding years of the women's liberation movement said,

It doesn't seem really probable that anyone would want to be no more than a housewife if all other avenues were open. Housework is uncreative, no matter what the mass media say about it in their relentless drive to sell a new cake mix or floor wax. Anyone who has ever done that kind of work for an extended period knows it is endless, repetitious drudgery

with—worst of all—no relevance to the larger
human community. It provides a pathetic
sense of being needed, of identity, to many
women. But anyone who thinks she feels
good as she surveys her kitchen after washing
the 146,789th batch of sparkling dishes isn't
being natural; she has literally lost her mind.[3]

Did women obtain their goal of sexual freedom, financial independence, and "equal rights" in the workplace? Yes, but not without sacrificing their loved ones. Since the 1970s the divorce rate has doubled. Abortion rates have skyrocketed, causing hundreds of thousands of unwarranted deaths each year. Pornography addiction, prostitution, sexual addiction, and sexually transmitted diseases are running rampant among millions of people. These same women have brought up like-minded daughters who have been raised by day care, MTV, and immoral television shows. Latchkey children are at the greatest risk of drug and alcohol addiction and involvement in crime. These social scourges have saddled the emerging generations with the legacy of an intolerable financial burden as our government attempts to combat the effects of personal irresponsibility.

Recapturing Biblical Womanhood

No matter how noble and fulfilling a woman's career outside the home may be, it is not an acceptable endeavor when it takes place at the expense of marriages and children. Why get married only to divorce within five years, which is the average time that a marriage lasts?[4] Why have children only to let the world raise them? God intended for marriages to last until "death do us part" and for children to be raised by both parents. Many families could do without some extras and live on one income in order to have the mother focus primarily on raising her children and investing in her marriage. The world's way screams for us to "keep up with the Joneses" and for women to adopt certain aspects of masculinity. But what our world truly needs is for couples to choose God's way instead of the world's way.

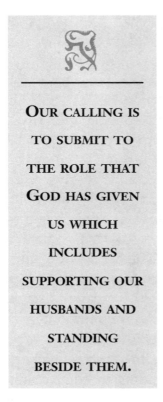

Our calling is to submit to the role that God has given us which includes supporting our husbands and standing beside them.

The feminist movement in no way bears sole responsibility for the moral decline of society. Still, we cannot ignore the tremendous role that it has played. In addition, the cure for our dysfunctional society will take place one marriage at a time, spreading throughout every city and state and to other nations. In the same way that Satan assigns specific demonic forces to a region, God himself has assigned you a territory—your marriage and your family, where you live. We must determine to fight for them with all the weapons available to us.

It is the responsibility of each of us to seek God's wisdom through his Word, comparing *our* core beliefs about marriage to *his* truth. We must also examine *the world's* concept of marriage in light of *God's* plan for marriage. These are the areas where we need to petition God for his help in order to learn and apply his truth in our marriages. Don't be misled. This is a spiritual battle in which Satan will not easily give up. He knows that if we walk in rebellion or independence from our mates, we will surely die spiritually. Satan will then succeed in his destruction of the family unit, which will certainly sabotage our children and their grandchildren for generations to come.

In Civil War literature "defeat in detail" means to defeat a force unit by unit, usually because the individual regiments or companies are not within supporting distance of one another. This is exactly what happens in a marriage where the wife continually usurps the authority of her husband. Looking back on the season when my children still lived at home, I can recall several examples of this. My husband would withhold permission for the children to participate in some activity, and I would undermine him by later allowing them to do what he had denied them permission to do. Or I would say things that subtly degraded him, like, "Well, you know how your father is; he's never really handled things like that well." Such situations may seem minor, but they teach our children that their father's authority is not valid, that they don't have to respect it. This "defeat in detail" frequently occurs in families where one parent does not support the other. Therein lies one more reason why children of divorce struggle so severely: It is because the united front that God created for them in parents is missing.

When we submit to our husbands' authority, we do so as unto God first and our husbands second. When we usurp it, we are telling God, and then our husbands, that we aren't going to listen. Our calling is to submit to the role that God has given us as wives and mothers, which includes supporting our husbands and standing beside them.

TO SUBMIT OR NOT TO SUBMIT

Are we always to submit, in every circumstance? Is it ever right *not* to submit to our husbands? In Colossians 3:18 we are told, "Wives, submit to your husbands, as is fitting in the Lord."

How is it fitting in the Lord? The meaning of the word *submit* is "to place in an orderly fashion, to place under." That does not mean that we mindlessly obey our husbands if they command us to do something that violates clear biblical teaching. We must, instead, weigh submission to our husbands against the Word of God, making it fitting in the Lord.

If we are living our lives in submission to God, sub-mission to our husbands will naturally occur. The only circumstance in which you would *not* submit would be if your husband requests you to do something that is against God's Word. I knew a woman who said that she started watching pornographic movies with her husband because he said that she had to submit to him and that's what he wanted to do. I knew another woman who endured years of physical abuse under the guise of submission. Both of these examples are not in submission to God because they are contrary to his Word. They are abusive distortions of God's Word, done for self-satisfaction.

When we submit to the biblically based leadership of our husbands, we are following the plan for wom-anhood that God designed at the beginning of creation. If we are married that means that we submit to the authority of our husbands as God intended. The danger against which we must guard is the tendency to seek to overthrow that authority, causing havoc in our marriages, our families, and, ultimately, our nation.

Sisters, "be self-controlled and alert" in this area of life. "Your enemy, the devil, prowls around like a roar-ing lion looking for someone to devour" (1 Peter 5:8). Resist him and stand firm in the faith.

Suffering and Spiritual Warfare

I consider that our present sufferings are not worth
comparing with the glory that will be revealed in us.

—Romans 8:18

*S*uffering, in all of its aspects, entered the world
when Adam and Eve disobeyed God in the garden of
Eden. As a result of this disobedience, they opened the
door to the consequences of suffering, including separation from God, pain in childbirth, and the cursing of
the ground, among other things. Like Adam and Eve,
many of us bring suffering upon ourselves through
our own sin. Suffering is not always the direct result
of sin, but we must realize that there are consequences
to our actions, and some involve suffering.

THE LAW OF THE HARVEST

Suffering people often ask me to intercede for them. My habit is to ask the Lord for insight into why the person is suffering. I do this in order to better pray for the person. Different types of suffering warrant different types of intercession. As a counselor, I have spent hundreds of hours listening to the hardships that people have endured. It is often the case that people are suffering at their own hand, as a result of their own choices. Many complain about their aching backs and hurting knees. It is sheer agony for some just to get out of bed. But they have never seemed to notice that they are excessively overweight. Their sinful overindulgence in food has brought them physical suffering. When a smoker gets lung cancer or an alcoholic gets cirrhosis of the liver, he is reaping the consequences of his own choices. It is the law of the harvest.

IT IS THROUGH PRAYER THAT WE BREAK THE SPIRITUAL WEBS THAT HAVE ENTANGLED US.

Regardless of what the sin is, there will be consequences physically, mentally, emotionally, and definitely spiritually. We are not to allow anything in life to become an idol to us. God warns us that he will tear down every idol that we place above him. To do so, he often uses the consequences of our behaviors. The alcoholic or drug addict loses his material possessions and health; the gossip loses friends and lives in chaos; the food addict's health deteriorates; the sex addict loses her marriage. Why are we surprised and angry that we suffer, since God warns us of the consequences of our rebellion? We expect him to keep his Word in other areas; we ought also to expect him to keep his Word in the area of behavioral consequences.

APPLY THE FIVE RS

When the Holy Spirit reveals through prayer an area of dependence on something other than God, our first response must be to take it to God in prayer, seeking repentance. To repent means to turn around, abandoning our previous behavior. We have previously addressed the cognitive or mental process of our behavior. (See chapter 5, "The Dynamics of Battle.") Remember that, once we have identified a false belief, we must come to a place of repentance where we honestly address our past behavior. It is through prayer that we break the spiritual webs that have entangled us. Let's review the "Five Rs" from the preceding chapter and apply them to ongoing idolatry.

1. **Recognize** that you are a sinner and have created an idol and placed it above God.
2. **Renounce** your involvement and addiction to this idol.

3. **Rebuke** the sin, casting it and the demonic hold that it has over you away from you.
4. **Receive** truth in its place—repeat what God's Word says about this idol.
5. **Rejoice** in the freedom that you now have in Christ.

The following is a sample prayer that can be used in order to overcome the besetting sin of gossip.

> Lord, I have a problem with gossiping. I recognize that I gossip because I want other people to like me and give me attention. I have relished this sin and have caused a lot of damage in my life and the lives of others. Please forgive me for slandering others in a vain attempt to meet my needs. I renounce the spirit of division that I have allowed to come into my life through gossip. I lay it at the foot of the cross. I rebuke Satan and his spirits of division, hatred, gossip, and manipulation that I have allowed into my life, and I command all you spirits in the name of Jesus to leave me now.
>
> You say in your Word, "A gossip betrays a confidence and separates close friends" and that "without gossip a quarrel dies down." So, I choose in the name of Jesus to be silent. I will walk in love, peace, and truth, speaking kindly of others, not taking part in gossip or slander. I also pray, Lord, that you will comfort me during the times when I am tempted to gossip, showing me

SUFFERING AND SPIRITUAL WARFARE

that my identity comes not from the attention of others, but from you. I receive your healing and love in this area in the name of Jesus.

Lord, I celebrate you and thank you that you have provided freedom for me from the pit of hell. I praise your holy name because you sacrificed everything so that I wouldn't have to live in the bondage of my sin. Praise the Lord. I thank you in Jesus' precious name.

You may adapt this prayer pattern to fit virtually any besetting sin. Besetting sins—strongholds—are usually present in our lives because of repeated behaviors that have ensnared us. By praying through the Five Rs, you will practice the cognitive process of behavior, but in a Spirit-led manner. You will recognize that you are not handling a situation appropriately. You will then examine the core belief or

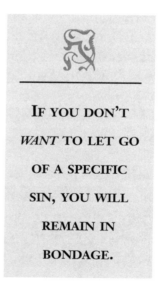

IF YOU DON'T WANT TO LET GO OF A SPECIFIC SIN, YOU WILL REMAIN IN BONDAGE.

thought that led you to the inappropriate behavior. Finally you will change the negative thought to a biblical one, accepting it as truth, and choose to walk according to God's Word.

Do You Want to Be Healed?

Part of my ministry is to spend time with three women during a three-hour process of prayer. My ministry partner and I take time with each woman separately in order to deal with a specific besetting sin. While my partner and I pray for one woman, the two other women are to pray silently for the woman with whom we are working. During one of our sessions one woman revealed to us a spirit of suicide that she had received years earlier. She had nurtured this spirit and relied on it to comfort her by providing an ungodly option whenever life became unmanageable. I wept while praying for her, rebuking the spirit and begging the Lord to grant her deliverance. As I fervently prayed, she finally came to the place where she was *willing* to release the spirit upon whom she had relied so long for comfort.

That lying spirit repeatedly told her that suicide was her only option. When she finally rejected that spirit, the spiritual bond that she had made with Satan was broken. She received the Holy Spirit in its place and has walked in freedom ever since. My point is this: the whole world may be praying for you, but if you don't *want* to let go of a specific sin, you will remain in bondage. My prayer for this woman was that her heart would soften and that she would understand that the suicide spirit was one of deception, not comfort. Satan had come to her as an angel of light, promising freedom from this world's troubles, but by nurturing that spirit and keeping suicide as an option, she was willingly enslaving herself to him.

I have often worked with women who wanted to *talk* about their problems but who did not want to work through them. It was as if, having fallen into a ditch, they asked for help to get out but then refused the helping hand that I extended to them. I'd say, "Here is my hand. Grab a hold of it and I will pull you out. Isn't that what you want?" That was often *not* what they wanted. Their reply was, in effect, "Well, I *thought* I wanted out. But since I've been down here I have been receiving so much attention. I like that. So I've changed my mind. I'd rather be in the ditch, gaining attention, than to be out where I might not get any." There are people who will go from therapist to therapist just to have someone listen to their problems but who are never willing to deal with any of them.

Jesus asked a crucial question of the recipient of one of his miracles. In John 5:6 he asked a man, "Do you want to get well?" Consider the person who gossips. In order for her to be healed of her sin and to live in freedom, she must be willing to give up the attention that she gets from gossiping. She must *want* to change.

What Others Intend for Evil, God Intends for Good

We also suffer due to the actions of others. I struggled for many years with the question of why God would allow me to be sexually abused as a child. Night and day I suffered from the effects of another person's sin. I began seeing a counselor when I was seventeen. It infuriated me one day when one of my counselors told me that Jesus was there with me when I was being abused and that he wept over what had happened. "Then why didn't he stop it?" I yelled. For many years, even as a believer, I struggled with this question. Then one day the Lord spoke to me through a teaching on suffering, and I realized that my abuser had a will also and that he chose to walk in disobedience to God and to violate me.

The abuse was a horrible experience, but I realized that God does not override his own spiritual laws. He has given us free will, and to take it away

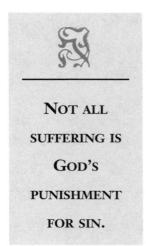

NOT ALL SUFFERING IS GOD'S PUNISHMENT FOR SIN.

from my perpetrator would have been contrary to *his* permissive will. (Permissive will meaning that God allows things to happen, rather than that he directly causes an event, which is his prescribed will.) I'm not saying that God decreed for me to be abused or that my perpetrator should have abused me. But God certainly knew that it would happen, and, according to Romans 8:28, regardless of

what that man did to me in his own will, God would ultimately use it to glorify himself. He would give me the strength to overcome that horrible experience and to proclaim his mercy and grace in the process. I wish that the abuse had never happened to me. But the resulting dependence upon God has brought me incredible intimacy with him that I would not trade for anything.

THE SOURCES OF OUR SUFFERING

Although we often try, we cannot control the behavior of other people. Wounded people wound people, and because we are all wounded, we all wound. There are only different degrees of injury. It is inevitable that we will hurt others, and they will hurt us.

Not all suffering is God's punishment for sin; neither is it necessarily the result of someone else's sin. In John 9:1–2 the disciples asked Jesus about a man who had been blind since birth. Was his handicap due to his sin, they inquired, or his parents' sin? Jesus replied that the man had been born blind "so that the work of God might be displayed in his life" (John 9:3). We sometimes suffer simply because in doing so we will glorify God.

Another cause of our suffering is the Enemy of our souls, Satan. Job was delivered into the hands of Satan in order to prove that Job was not serving God simply because God had blessed him. Job knew that his suffering was temporary and that it would cease at some point in the future. Waiting for Christ's full and final redemption gave him hope. He said, "I know that my Redeemer lives, and that in the end he will stand upon the earth. And after my skin has been destroyed, yet

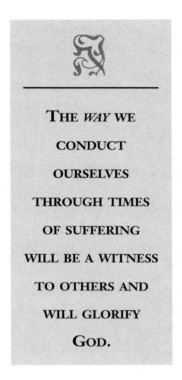

THE *WAY* WE CONDUCT OURSELVES THROUGH TIMES OF SUFFERING WILL BE A WITNESS TO OTHERS AND WILL GLORIFY GOD.

in my flesh I will see God; I myself will see him with my own eyes—I, and not another. How my heart yearns within me!" (Job 19:25–27).

Job knew that the Redeemer who had purchased him from the slavery of sin had not forgotten him, even though he was suffering tremendously. Jesus encourages us not to let our hearts be troubled but to trust in God. He tells us that our trials will someday end, at which point we will be with him forever. The cognitive or mental process we discussed earlier is vital here, and we can use it to help us work through our response when difficulties arise.

Regardless of *why* we suffer, the *way* we conduct ourselves through times of suffering will be a witness to others and will glorify God. Furthermore, we should remember that Jesus was made perfect through suffering (see Heb. 2:10, 5:8) and that his suffering enabled him to understand our struggles and weaknesses. In the same way, God calls upon us to share in Christ's sufferings. When God placed on our sinless Savior the sins of the world, his intense suffering was both physical and spiritual. We see a glimpse of his agony on the cross at Calvary when Jesus cried out, *"Eloi, Eloi, lama sabachthani?"* meaning "My God, my God, why have you forsaken me?" (See Matt. 27:46.)

THE PERFECTING POWER OF STRUGGLES

When Jesus told his disciples to strive for the same perfection as God the Father, he meant that God is the standard by which we should measure everything. The apostle Paul committed to preaching and teaching believers until they became perfect in Christ (see Col. 1:28), which means *mature* in Christ. It is often through suffering that a believer develops perfection, or maturity. (See James 1:2–4.)

The apostle Peter wrote,

> If you suffer for doing good and you endure it, this is commendable before God. To this you were called, because Christ suffered for you, leaving you an example, that you should follow in his steps.... But even if you should suffer for what is right, you are blessed.... It is better, if it is God's will, to suffer for doing good than for doing evil.
> (1 Peter 2:20–22; 3:14,17)

We are to endure, just as Christ endured. Let's consider the butterfly. It is a tremendous struggle for these insects to reach adulthood. As they labor and stretch to free themselves from their chrysalides, the process forces blood from their small bodies into their wings. Once the blood is thoroughly dispersed, the wings expand until they are large and strong enough to support the weight of the butterfly. If anything interferes with the process, the butterfly's wings will never be strong enough to support its body.

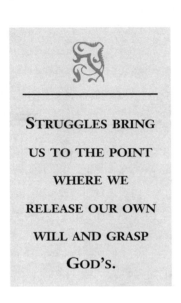

STRUGGLES BRING US TO THE POINT WHERE WE RELEASE OUR OWN WILL AND GRASP GOD'S.

Our sanctification involves a continual struggle between our flesh and our spirits. If we do not struggle, we will never learn to grow spiritually. Struggles bring us to the point where we release our own will and grasp God's. It is in our weakness that we become dependent upon Christ, enabling him to be our strength. Thus, through our suffering we become perfect—mature in Christ.

Consider the ten plagues that the Lord visited upon Egypt; they were all designed to reveal to the Egyptians that the Lord is God. (See Ex. 10:2.) The same is true in our lives. There is a purpose and a plan for all our suffering. It is not random or meant to harm us, but to draw us closer to him—to teach us, correct us, and change us, so that we, like the butterfly, will undergo a complete metamorphosis and become Christlike.

How can we maintain the perspective of Christ, especially when we know that painful trials are a certainty? We begin with the realization that we are not mere human beings. We are body *and* spirit. Therefore, we are able to fight against the principalities, powers, and rulers of this dark world.

Human beings who do not know Jesus Christ do not have God's Spirit in them. Consequently, they struggle in worldly ways. It is all they know. They battle flesh against flesh (against one another) and flesh against spirit (against God). Believers possess the Spirit of God within them. However, we believers also have to choose how we will engage in spiritual battle: either in the flesh (the sinful nature) or the spirit. In his book *The Believer's Prayer Life*, Andrew Murray wrote, "Scripture teaches us that there are but two conditions possible for the Christian. One is a walk according to the Spirit, the other a walk according to 'the flesh.' These two powers are in irreconcilable conflict with each other."[1]

The believer has the power to choose which way to fight: in the flesh or in the spirit. Unbelievers don't have a choice. They do not have the Holy Spirit to help them overcome trials and tribulations; and therefore, they are forced to walk in the flesh. Believers have the Holy Spirit living in them. We also possess natural strengths and weaknesses. In his book *The Handbook for Spiritual Warfare*, Dr. Ed Murphy concedes, "We all have three things. We have strengths, limitations, and flaws.... To know my limitations is as important as knowing my strengths."[2] We must be familiar with all three of these, because our enemy, the Devil, is certainly familiar with them.

Whenever I, as a new believer, encountered difficult circumstances, other Christians often told me that the battle I was struggling with had already been won. "If that is true," I wondered, "then why am I struggling so much?" After wrestling with God over the matter, I finally realized that I experienced pain and difficulty when at least one of several conditions was present: (1) I wasn't walking in God's promises of victory; (2) I was relying on myself, the old sinful nature; or (3) I wasn't protecting myself with God's armor.

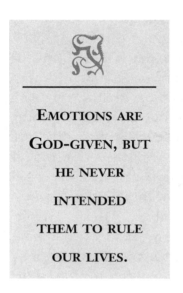

EMOTIONS ARE GOD-GIVEN, BUT HE NEVER INTENDED THEM TO RULE OUR LIVES.

When we rely on our own wisdom, our own ways, and our own resources, we are dealing with the flesh—the sinful nature. But we do not have the power in the old man (the flesh) to fight a battle. The flesh is weak, old, tired, and useless. The only thing that it ever brought us was bondage. But we have unlimited power available to us through the Spirit of

God. The same power that raised Jesus from the dead resides in us. If we rely on the Holy Spirit, we can overcome any temptation. God promises that he will not allow us to be tempted beyond our capability to resist. He promises a way out of every temptation.

The Importance of Perspective and Expectations

One of the greatest gifts that a new believer receives from the Lord is a new perspective. To be able to see situations and people from his point of view awakens our spirits to respond in a godly manner. If the Holy Spirit guides our perception of others, as well as the manner in which we handle difficult circumstances, we will live in freedom, with an easy yoke and a burden that's light.

Such a change of perspective enables us to detach ourselves emotionally from the situation, to examine the facts, to see the truth through God's eyes, and then to allow our emotions to respond in a godly and healthy manner. Emotions are God-given, but he never intended them to rule our lives. Christ offers us self-control. What we think about the people around us or our circumstances often determines our emotional and physical responses. That is why it is crucial that we not only learn God's Word but also apply it to our lives. When Jesus was attacked by Satan, he used the Word to protect himself. We must do the same.

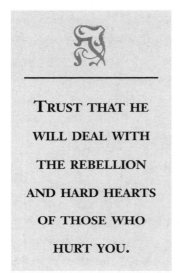

TRUST THAT HE WILL DEAL WITH THE REBELLION AND HARD HEARTS OF THOSE WHO HURT YOU.

In turn, we must learn to detach from individuals who seek, consciously or unconsciously, to tear us down spiritually. Instead, we must choose to associate with people who will encourage our walk with Christ. There are two types of people in the world: believers and unbelievers. We ought never to expect unbelievers to act like believers. They look at life from a worldly perspective. They respond from a worldview that is the opposite of the believer's and will not respond to events from a spiritual standpoint. Scripture tells us that Christianity is foolish to those who are perishing. Our ways may, in fact, be offensive to them, but remember that even Jesus himself offended the Pharisees with truth. We expect unbelievers to behave as unbelievers.

We also should be able to expect fellow believers to act like believers. They will often disappoint us. The man who led me to the Lord told me that the greatest hurt that I would ever receive would be from other believers. He cautioned me about putting other believers on a pedestal. He was correct. Had I listened to his advice, I would have saved myself a great deal of pain and anguish. We may expect believers to behave as believers, but they sometimes act worse than unbelievers.

Our *disappointment* in another person is determined by our *expectation* of him. We expect believers to act like believers, and we are disappointed when they do not. But if we understand that they too are in process, we can forgive them more easily when they let us down.

Anyone who has been a member of the body of Christ for a long time has undoubtedly experienced conflict with another believer. Keep in mind that we are all in the process of growth, and none of us— except God—is perfect. He is the only one who will not leave you, forsake you, hang you out to dry, gossip about you, or slander you. He also says, "Vengeance is mine" (Rom. 12:19 NKJV). Trust that he will deal with the rebellion and hard hearts of those who hurt you and are not repentant. That is *his* job, not *yours*.

Dependency Outside of Christ

My salvation and my honor depend on God;
he is my mighty rock, my refuge.

—Psalm 61:7

J grew up in a home where I watched my mother submit to a man who terribly abused her. She had no voice, no authority, and no value in his eyes. She learned to tolerate whatever he handed to her, surviving some of the most horrific abuse I've ever seen.

Instead of confronting my father about his numerous affairs, his abusive behavior, and his reckless spending, she silently endured it. She didn't talk to anyone else about it; instead, she believed that she could not survive apart from him. My mother had no idea that she was enabling my father's behavior and playing a part in her own physical, emotional, and spiritual deterioration. She was also by her example teaching her children to do the same.

CODEPENDENCE AND IDOLATRY

Such is the life of a codependent. The word is a combination of two words: *co*, meaning "with" or "associated with" the action of another, and *dependent*, meaning a reliance on another person or thing for support or existence. This definition is at the core of idolatry.

Some women actually idolize their mates. For others, it is their children whom they turn into idols. For still others, it is their careers, homes, money, self, or even their youthfulness. This kind of reliance on another person or thing for support is offensive to a holy and righteous God.

It is not unusual for a woman to believe that her mate is that one special person who will provide all the love and security that she needs. Nor is it abnormal for a mother to believe that she should provide all the love and security that her child needs. These thoughts, while

NO ONE PERSON CAN MEET ALL YOUR NEEDS FOR LOVE AND SECURITY.

they paint a beautiful picture, are lies. No one person can meet all your needs for love and security; neither can you meet all the needs of love and security for others.

When we have an unhealthy dependence on someone, such as a mate, parent, child, or even friend, we are placing that person and her needs and wants above Christ. To make matters worse, as we engage in the compulsion to rescue, control, or fix another person, we put ourselves in the position of being that person's savior. God never meant for us to fix other people. To think that we are capable of doing so outside of Christ is idolatry of self.

GOD NEVER MEANT FOR US TO FIX OTHER PEOPLE.

As the chaplain of a prison that housed over fourteen hundred inmates, I saw parents and inmates continually playing these roles. Parents would lose their homes because they put them up for bond money for a child who simply continued to use drugs and then skipped out on his court dates. Wives would lie to the courts so that their abusive husbands would be released from jail, only to be blamed and beat up some more upon their husbands' release because the husbands held their wives responsible for their initial incarceration.

Who is to say that the drug-addicted child and the abusive husband might not be humbled and turn to

Christ if we refused to interfere, letting God deal with them? I have often asked, once a person begins to change, what the turning point was. The all-too-frequent answer? "When my family quit rescuing me!"

THE ROOTS AND THE CONSEQUENCES

Codependency generally emanates from unmet childhood needs for things such as love, acceptance, and security in primary relationships—as with parents, guardians, spouses, or children. Children raised in unhealthy homes learn to discern unspoken messages. For example, the child raised in an alcoholic home

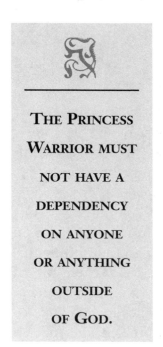

THE PRINCESS
WARRIOR MUST
NOT HAVE A
DEPENDENCY
ON ANYONE
OR ANYTHING
OUTSIDE
OF GOD.

learns to identify that when Mom is irritable and edgy, it's because she's worried that Dad is out drinking the rent money away again. The child can also tell whether or not Dad's been drinking, just by reading the expression on his face when he walks into the room. This identification of events should not be confused with spiritual discernment. It is a learned pattern for survival purposes.

The problems of the codependent are many. They have a heightened sense of responsibility, and they willingly wear the heavy coat of guilt, shame, hurt, anger, and loneliness in a complex and desperate quest to avoid abandonment. They fail to realize that only God can banish forever the fear of abandonment.

THE WAY TO HEALING

The Princess Warrior must not have a dependency on anyone or anything outside of God, for he is a jealous God and has vowed to tear down every idol that we put in his place. Healing from codependency requires confession to God that something or someone has taken his place. We must accept his forgiveness and ongoing scrutiny of our relationships with other people. Although it is, at times, certainly appropriate to receive godly counsel and guidance through professional counselors or trusted friends, it's important to remember that our dependence must be on God and that lasting change comes as we grow in him, even when he uses his children in our lives.

Consider the following verses:

My salvation and my honor depend on God;
he is my mighty rock, my refuge. (Ps. 62:7)

Trust in him at all times, O people; pour out your hearts to him, for God is our refuge. (Ps. 62:8)

Each one should test his own actions. Then
he can take pride in himself, without comparing himself to somebody else, for each
one should carry his own load. (Gal. 6:4–5)

Cast all your anxiety on him because he
cares for you. (1 Peter 5:7)

In the same way, count yourselves dead to
sin but alive to God in Christ Jesus. Therefore
do not let sin reign in your mortal body so
that you obey its evil desires. (Rom. 6:11–12)

Choose several of these verses, memorize them,
and recite them daily. You will find that as you take
captive every thought to the Word of God you will
begin a journey of healing and freedom from a life of
codependency.

My Story of Warfare and Salvation

Think of me as a fellow-patient in the same hospital who,
having been admitted a little earlier, could give some advice.

—C. S. Lewis

*T*hroughout this book I've shared bits and pieces of my own story. A book about spiritual warfare must include personal experience and knowledge of what it is like to be on the front lines of battle. There are some crucial elements about my life that I want to share with you: Satan's specific and direct attacks on my life, as well as how God has conquered them and used them for his glory.

Children of God have a unique spirit about them and are identifiable to Satan. Scripture tells us that God has sanctified us; he has set us apart for a unique purpose, even before we were formed in our mothers' wombs. (See Jer. 1:5.) Satan attempts not so much to make us hate our Creator, but to make us forget him through preoccupation with the world's treasures or pain. Such was the case in my life.

The Gauntlet Is Thrown

My mother was virtually an orphan during her formative years. She was raised by numerous family members and was in the state child welfare system as my grandmother went from man to man in her failed attempts to find love. When my mother was seventeen she was living in California with her aunt, who worked at a restaurant not far from where they lived. My mother would often walk down to meet her aunt as she was getting off of work so they could walk home together.

Satan was not pleased with my survival.

My father was a twenty-one-year-old cook who, when he saw my mother one afternoon, asked her out. He got permission from her aunt to take her on a date one evening, and she had a good time, agreeing to date him again. On her second date, however, he raped her at gunpoint. When she failed to return home that night, her aunt called the police.

The authorities eventually found my mother at my father's apartment and took her to a girls' reform school. My father was taken into police custody, pending charges of statutory rape. When my grandmother heard the news, she drove to the town where my mother lived, arrived at the police station, and confronted my father. She gave him two options: marry my mother or face a charge of statutory rape.

Prior to this my father had served six months in jail for stealing a car. In order to avoid more jail time, he chose—with my grandmother's blessing—to marry my mother. In this way our twisted branch in the family tree—my heritage—began. My older brother, Danny, was born within a year. Shortly thereafter my mother found herself pregnant with me. Thus began the attack on my life.

After discovering that she was pregnant my mother began to have severe abdominal pain and was rushed to the hospital. She was told by the doctor that I was a tubal pregnancy and that she would require surgery to dispose of the embryo (me) in order to save her own life. She agreed to do so, but God had different plans, intervening in a way that only he could. He knew the plans that he had for me, plans for good and not for evil, a plan to prosper my growth, not hinder it. (See Jer. 29:11.) Miraculously, when the doctor performed the surgery he discovered that I had moved from the fallopian tubes into my mother's uterus without any problems. I was born eight months later. Two years later my mother gave birth to my younger brother, Dale.

Satan was not pleased with my survival. He had tried unsuccessfully to take me out of the picture. Therefore, shortly after I was born he came into my life through the evil desires of others who stole my innocence through all types of abuse. I was sexually violated by two family members and a neighbor, and my father was physically, emotionally, and verbally abusive to me. To further complicate the issue, my family was steeped in various aspects of the occult.

THE BATTLE INTENSIFIES

Despite this twisted and flawed foundation, I had an interest in God. And because of that innate interest, I asked a lot of questions that went unanswered. In an attempt to stop me from asking questions, my mother started putting my brothers and me on the big, blue Bible Baptist Church bus that passed by our house every Sunday. Dressed in our best school clothes, with a quarter to put in the offering plate at Sunday school, my brothers and I would climb up onto that bus.

I loved going to Sunday school, and one of my teachers, a young, Spirit-filled college student, gave me a star for memorizing an entire chapter of the Bible: Psalm 23. Unfortunately, that teacher taught only two Sundays every month. The rest of my church experience consisted of clowns and Kool-Aid, childhood games, and chasing one another between the pews. Before long we stopped going. After all, we could play like that at home without having to dress up.

Somewhere along the way my maternal grandmother got radically saved and moved from one end of the spiritual spectrum to the other. She abandoned her depraved life and began living wholeheartedly for God. She married a godly man who would become instrumental in my conversion many years later.

My family considered my grandmother a religious fanatic because she continually quoted the Bible. The conviction of her words was overpowering to my parents, who lived in a world of deceit. Our deception caused us all to be thankful that she lived a thousand miles away. My grandparents would occasionally visit, and one summer I developed a very special relationship with my grandfather, Neil. He was a gentle soul with great wisdom, love, and a soft spot for his only granddaughter. He hugged me a lot and often told me that he loved me. He would frequently talk about the Lord, but in a nonabrasive manner, sharing stories that gave me the impression that he really *knew* Jesus.

When I was twelve years old, my father trusted Christ as his Savior and began taking the family to church. The abuse stopped, and my father began spending time at home playing games with the family and reading the Bible. We went to church as a family, spending time with other Christians and even sharing dinner several times at the pastor's home. Although I hadn't made a personal commitment to Christ, I saw the change in my father's life, and it was a testimony to God's saving power.

My father disappeared six months later on a three-week drinking binge. When he returned home, he cursed the church, Christians, and God. As I lay in my bedroom sobbing, I could hear him insisting that it had all been an act, that he never really meant anything that he had said or done. The abuse resumed. Shortly thereafter, I attempted suicide for the first time.

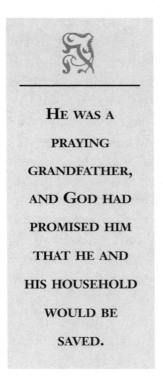

HE WAS A PRAYING GRANDFATHER, AND GOD HAD PROMISED HIM THAT HE AND HIS HOUSEHOLD WOULD BE SAVED.

After the first attempt I found other ways to hide my pain with drugs, alcohol, sex, and the occult. A couple of months later I watched helplessly as my father, in a drunken rage, raped my mother. In pain, I rebelled at every opportunity, picking fights—both verbally and physically—with my father.

From there I wholeheartedly threw myself into the arms of the world, further entangling myself in the web of its deception. Self-defeating behavior ruled my life until, at twenty years of age, I found myself sitting in a prison cell serving a six-month sentence. I was divorced with two children, and, worst of all, I had no hope. I had tried to commit suicide multiple times in an attempt to end the pain in which I was drowning. While I was in jail several churches sent ministry teams to minister to the inmates, but I rejected them along with the message of hope that they offered.

When I left prison I moved to California to go to school and to make something of my life. During my years there, my grandfather, who was so influential in my preteen years, died. When I heard that he was dying of cancer, I drove more than two hundred miles to sit at his bedside. As I wept uncontrollably, he promised me that he'd see me again someday in heaven. While I nodded my head in agreement, I had no concept of salvation and certainly no hope of going to heaven. But he was a praying grandfather, and God had promised him that he and his household would be saved—including that rebellious little girl in a grown-up body, the one who hated and blamed God for all her problems.

After completing my education, I moved to Nashville, Tennessee, to pursue a career in counseling and music publishing. I began counseling for the YWCA in a home for troubled girls. I was twenty-four years old, and for the first time in my life I was on my own, functioning in a relatively healthy manner. But I was still dissatisfied.

The War Is Won

I have always loved to exercise, and at that time I regularly ran three miles a day. My apartment was in a high-rise complex located downtown and sandwiched between shops and businesses. One day as I ran I reflected on how far I'd traveled in my short life. I thought I was happy ... but was I?

"You *should* be," I told myself as I ran, dodging businessmen in suits. "You have everything you've ever wanted—your own home, a career, and money in the bank. What more could you want?" I quickly dismissed my feelings of dissatisfaction as ungratefulness, and I looked for a more positive thought to ponder. I laughed as Psalm 23, which I had memorized as a young girl, popped into my head. *Nevertheless,* I thought, *it's better to reflect on those verses than on my past.*

I nonchalantly repeated the oft-spoken verse as I ran. "The Lord is my shepherd; I shall not want." I crossed a busy street, pausing for a brief moment, and then continued. "He maketh me to lie down in green pastures." I saw my apartment building in the distance and picked up the pace of both my running and my words. "He leadeth me beside the still waters."

I was running hard at this point. Sweat was dripping down my back, and my short hair was matted to my head. As I stepped onto my three-mile mark in the parking lot of my apartment building I shouted, "He restoreth my soul!" I bent over in exhilarating pain from the workout. "He restoreth my soul," I said out loud, more softly this time, but I continued to repeat it. "He restoreth my soul, he restoreth my soul."

As I said these words, something stirred inside of me. It was as if a lightbulb had turned on, exposing a sacred secret that I'd known all along yet had hidden even from myself. I hadn't prayed to God in years. "What is the point of prayer," I'd ask, "unless you are in trouble?" But something inside kept nudging at me.

"Behold, I stand at the door and knock" (Rev. 3:20 NKJV).

"God," I prayed silently, "that's the answer. My soul is broken, and that's why I'm not happy. If you really are up there, will you restore my soul?"

At that moment it suddenly became clear to me: if God originally made the soul, then he should be able to restore it!

As powerful as that moment was, I immediately let go of it and went about my day. God, however, would not let go. Within a week I was introduced to an evangelical Christian who would, in the months to come, lead me to the Lord and disciple me. God is faithful, and he knew the innermost desire of my heart, which was restoration. At that moment my heart became one with his. He too was seeking restoration. He spoke to me, the unbeliever, in an attempt to draw me into his kingdom. He initiated the contact, which became a romance that has led to twelve years of continual transformation.

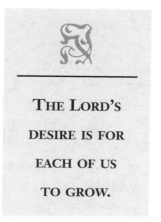

THE LORD'S DESIRE IS FOR EACH OF US TO GROW.

THE WOUNDED BECOMES THE WARRIOR

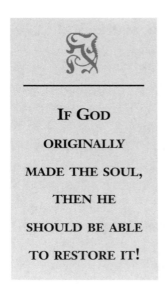

IF GOD ORIGINALLY MADE THE SOUL, THEN HE SHOULD BE ABLE TO RESTORE IT!

As real as his ministry of reconciliation seems in the biblical accounts, God became *personally* real to me. He is now my everything, the focus of my love and admiration. It is with great honor that I worship and serve him. Jesus told his disciples in Mark 10:29–30 that anyone who relinquished everything to follow him would receive it back a hundredfold. God always multiplies the blessings when he renews a relationship. Through the acceptance of Christ as our Savior, he replaces the unbeliever's life with a more powerful, majestic, and glorious one than we could ever have imagined. His promises of restoration are true. The key to all of this is our removal of ourselves from the throne of our lives and the placing of our heavenly Father there, where he belongs.

I was a slave to sin, as well as to the master of sin, Satan. Deliverance from this master required payment of a ransom. When I asked for freedom, Jesus rescued me, providing redemption through his death. Deliverance from my sin resulted in freedom.

During my life as an unbeliever I sought redemption through self-help books, religion, secular counseling, treatment centers, and medication. They were just Band-Aids on my gaping wounds. None of them brought true healing; they simply lacked the healing power that I needed. God can certainly use such resources as counseling, books, and even medication. But none of them, by themselves, can truly heal.

Simply giving a name or a diagnosis to a wound does not heal it. Calling cancer by its name does not bring healing to the body. It is just a label, and labels help to only *identify* the wound. Doctors *treat*, but Jesus *heals*. The same is true of medications, psychiatrists, counselors, self-help books, and, yes, even pastors. They *treat*; Jesus *heals*.

I spent years in therapy as the result of childhood abuse and self-inflicted abuse as an adolescent and young adult. I've read many self-help books and attended hundreds of secular seminars on how to attain healing, peace, and joy. In doing so, I eventually learned to function in a somewhat healthy manner in a dysfunctional world. Nothing

THROUGH THE ACCEPTANCE OF CHRIST AS OUR SAVIOR, HE REPLACES THE UNBELIEVER'S LIFE WITH A MORE POWERFUL, MAJESTIC, AND GLORIOUS ONE THAN WE COULD EVER HAVE IMAGINED.

I tried, however, brought even a glimpse of complete healing in any area of my life. You might say that I changed from an informal and disordered garden to a formal and organized garden, but I sensed that there was something more—I just didn't know what.

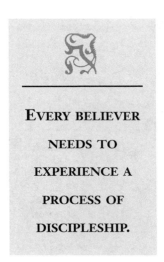

EVERY BELIEVER NEEDS TO EXPERIENCE A PROCESS OF DISCIPLESHIP.

When I became a believer on November 2, 1993, my reconstruction began from within, and it continues to this day, transforming a garden overrun by weeds into a temple wherein the Holy Spirit resides. Although the remodeling is not yet complete, the Holy Spirit is the contractor and oversees every step of the building process. The goal is for the temple within to reflect perfectly the image of Christ. It is tragic when developing believers never have the opportunity to reach maturity in Christ, fully and perfectly reflecting his image.

The Lord's desire is for each of us to grow, become mature, and to bear fruit—"some a hundredfold, some sixty, some thirty" (Matt. 13:8 NKJV). There are many times, however, when immature believers experience an arrested development.

As the chaplain for a private prison that housed more than fourteen hundred inmates, I was allowed to hold one evangelistic outreach per month; this was granted to me by the gracious warden of the facility.

As word leaked out about this opportunity, I had a backlog of churches and ministries signed up to share with the inmates. Every month the same scenario played out: A church or ministry would come in and conduct worship and prayer, present a speaker, and then extend an invitation to accept Christ. Every month hundreds of inmates would commit their lives to the Lord. The pastors and leaders walked out of the prison on a spiritual cloud. The inmates, however, went back to their cells and were forgotten. There was little or no follow-up, no discipleship, and no contact.

The new Christian, momentarily soothed by the washing of the Word, was left to drown in stale, cold water. There were simply too many people and too little time to complete the necessary follow-up after the initial investment from the church.

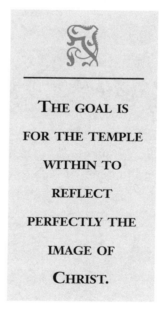

THE GOAL IS FOR THE TEMPLE WITHIN TO REFLECT PERFECTLY THE IMAGE OF CHRIST.

The next month another church would arrive, present another program, and the inmates would go through the process all over again. I knew inmates who had received salvation thirty times but had never been discipled. Unfortunately, this is also common in churches. A message of salvation is given without discipleship or follow-up, and new believers—often

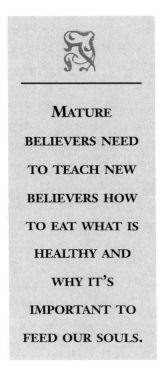

MATURE BELIEVERS NEED TO TEACH NEW BELIEVERS HOW TO EAT WHAT IS HEALTHY AND WHY IT'S IMPORTANT TO FEED OUR SOULS.

fiercely attacked by the Enemy—walk away from their newfound faith feeling defeated and labeling the experience as emotional rather than substantive.

The part of the evangelistic process that was missing was painfully clear: follow-up and discipleship. Every believer needs to experience a process of discipleship in order to gain a strong foundational understanding of who she is in Christ. This is not to imply that everyone who is discipled is guaranteed not to fall away from his faith. But when a building has a strong foundation, it is much more likely to withstand the earthquakes and storms of life. Jesus tells us in Matthew 7:24–27,

> Therefore whoever hears these sayings of Mine, and does them, I will liken him to a wise man who built his house on the rock: and the rain descended, the floods came, and the winds blew and beat on that house; and it did not fall, for it was founded on the rock.
>
> But everyone who hears these sayings of Mine, and does not do them, will be like a foolish man who built his house on the sand:

and the rain descended, the floods came, and
the winds blew and beat on that house; and
it fell. And great was its fall. (NKJV)

New Christians are like babies, and babies cannot initially feed themselves. They begin with breast milk. Even
when a child graduates to solid food he can make a real
mess. Have you ever watched a baby feed herself *solid*
food for the first time? It's everywhere: on the floor,
walls, highchair, and child! This is a picture of the new
believer who needs assistance with his newfound faith.
Mature believers need to teach new believers how to eat
what is healthy and why it's important to feed our souls.

Keep in mind that it is not always the fault of pastors
and leaders when individuals
do not achieve fruitfulness.
Some people attempt to
manipulate the world around
them rather than to make
changes from within. Making
internal changes, however,
will have the most profound
and lasting effect on the
world around us.

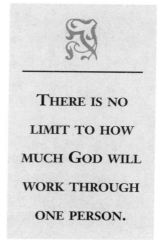

**THERE IS NO
LIMIT TO HOW
MUCH GOD WILL
WORK THROUGH
ONE PERSON.**

Psychiatric wards, hospi-
tals, prisons, and even the
body of Christ are full of people who try to manipulate
the outside world but refuse to change on the inside.
They resist change, defy growth, and demand others to
conform to their perception of reality, which in turn

draws people around them into the bondage that has captivated them. These individuals lack one of the two necessities of faith: *trust* or *belief*. In my experience, the missing link is most often *trust*. They have been so wounded in life that they refuse to trust anyone, even God. They tear apart the body of Christ rather than build it up. They are critical and demanding, with little or no desire to examine their own hearts. As long as they focus on the sins of others, they don't have to face their own.

When we realize that God is active in every moment of our existence, from our conception to our birth, from our salvation to our death and the afterlife, daily events will fall into place and all of life will take on a spiritual significance. When I can demonstrate to those whom I counsel that God has not forsaken them but has orchestrated their very existence, they see life differently, through God's perspective.

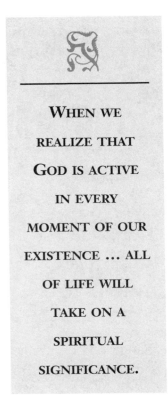

WHEN WE REALIZE THAT GOD IS ACTIVE IN EVERY MOMENT OF OUR EXISTENCE ... ALL OF LIFE WILL TAKE ON A SPIRITUAL SIGNIFICANCE.

There is no limit to how much God will work through one person and how much glory he will receive when he finds one person whose heart is sold out to him. Shortly after my conversion I was blessed to be instrumental in leading my younger brother, Dale, to the Lord. He now serves as a worship leader among his church family in Oregon. He has married and is raising two children as unto the Lord. My brother Dale, after hearing the title of this book, shared with me a song about spiritual warfare that he had recently written. The lyrics to that song are included at the end of this chapter.

My older brother, Danny, also a songwriter, has recently come to know Jesus as well. In the fall of 2003 my mother accepted Jesus as her Savior. What a blessing it has been to watch God restore my family to him! There are still members who have yet to embrace God's kingdom, but I am praying and believing God's Word to be true and that my entire family will be saved.

WARRIOR
by Dale Daugherty

I know you're tired and scared
And the wound is cut real deep
But the favor of the Lord is on you
For the Devil, that spells defeat
Day by day goes by
Never seeing what's the truth
There's a spiritual war upon us
And the Lord is calling for you

Chorus
Warrior, warrior,
You are a warrior,
The Lord is calling for you
The Lord is calling for you

Young and old unite
Standing side by side
Preparing for the battle
Preparing for the fight
Training every day
Praying day and night
Mold my heart for battle
Lord, prepare me to fight

Chorus

The time for battle is now
The Devil's on the field
By the power of God's Word
We will crush him with our heels
The army of the beast
Is trying with all their might
Never understanding
They've already lost the fight … because we're

Chorus

The battle's done and gone
Only blood stains the ground
The seven-headed beast
Is dead and lost his crowns
A trumpet sounds aloud
Declaring victory
Almighty is our Lord
The first and last is he

He's a warrior, a warrior,
He's a warrior, declaring victory

READERS' GUIDE

*For Personal Reflection or
Group Discussion*

Readers' Guide

*P*erhaps you have wondered what it takes to experience the "life of victory" that we hear so much about. We hear the testimonies that others share about their miracles and wonderful answers to prayer. The solutions sound familiar but never seem to work for us. There are times we question who we are and why we struggle with wounds from the past and besetting sins in the present. We have prayed for deliverance from the shackles that bind us. However, the chains remain, rusty and grimy, but as strong as ever. The search for "victory" seems as promising as a search for a four-leaf clover in a patch of poison ivy. Kind of a disincentive for any serious future explorations.

We end up settling into a quiet life of dissatisfaction and defeat. These questions periodically rise to the surface of our consciousness, "Does it really have to be this way? Must I continue to plod along in the same patterns of spiritual doldrums?" We have nearly given up on even the thought of buying another spiritual self-help book. But this book delivers the hope for which you yearn.

As you work through the following readers' guide, ask yourself the same question Jesus asked the paralyzed man by the pool of Bethesda, "Do you want to get well?" (John 5:6). If you do, direct your thoughts to the questions that accompany each of the chapters you will experience. Then personalize the prayer that you find at the end of each chapter's questions.

You will undoubtedly find that some of the chapters uncover wounds and bruises from a painful past. Some may even trigger memories of events that have remained long forgotten under layers of anger, dependency, and depression. One of the great lies with which Satan wants to hold you captive is the belief that your life can never be better. Learn to use the methods and principles described in this book to analyze the way you make decisions. It may even be wise, as you uncover issues from your past, to engage the services of a qualified licensed counselor with experience in dealing with issues of abuse, addictions, anger, or depression.

A productive course of action may be to study each chapter and its related Scripture passages in the context of a small group. Read the chapter and work through the questions yourself in preparation for your discussion. You will notice that some of the initial questions may serve as icebreakers or as warm-ups to deeper contemplation and discussion. Subsequent questions, however, will dig more deeply; they may even evoke responses that will speak from places of pain and distress you would rather ignore. I urge you, however, to press through the pain to find your victory in the Lord.

As you personalize and apply the principles in *Engaging the Enemy*, you will be able to take your stand in your identity as both a daughter and princess of the Lord himself. Your spiritual armor will rest securely upon you, preparing you for battle and enabling you to take your stand against the Devil's schemes and lies. You will learn how to utilize the power of the Holy Spirit who walks alongside every believer. Your marriage will become stronger, and you will interact in a more godly and Christ-honoring way with your husband. If you are unmarried, you will learn lessons essential for becoming the godly wife in any possible future marriage. And if God calls you to a life of single service on his behalf, you will be able to do so with boldness, confidence, and in godly dependence on him.

Open your heart to learn from the author as she shares with you the agony she experienced throughout the formative and early adult years of her life. Seek to be as open with your sisters in Christ—perhaps those who are in your study group—and take the risk to be vulnerable and transparent with them. Then together you will be able to "press through" toward victory as the *princess warriors* God has called and empowered you to be.

Press through, Princess Warrior!

Chapter One:
Our Identity: Daughter and Princess Warrior

1. What are the earliest and happiest moments from your childhood? Who were you with, and under what circumstances?

2. What are your saddest moments from childhood? Who were you with, and under what circumstances?

3. Jesus describes in Matthew 11:29–30 his "easy yoke." What are the words to describe the "yoke" you bear?

4. Hemingway wrote in his book *A Farewell to Arms* that "the world breaks everyone, and afterwards some are strong in the broken places." How have your experiences of brokenness made you stronger?

5. How would you describe yourself? Complete the sentence, "I see myself as

_____.

6. Now take your Bible and read the following passages: Romans 8:29; Psalm 139:16; Colossians 3:9–10. Complete this sentence: "God sees me as

_____."

7. When Ephesians 1:13–14 says you have been "sealed" by the Holy Spirit, it means that you now belong to God. That same Holy Spirit is a "deposit" or "pledge of your inheritance" guaranteeing your life with Christ. What does that truth communicate about your destiny and inheritance with Jesus Christ?

MY PRAYER

Lord, I thank you today for the memories that I carry from my early life, both the good and the sad memories. I thank you for the broken places in my life. You have promised to make me strong in the broken places. Thank you for the promise that you can replace my heavy burden with one that is light and useful for your purpose in my life. Help me to see myself today as one whom you call your "princess" and your "daughter." In Jesus' name, amen.

CHAPTER TWO:
QUEEN ESTHER: A BIBLICAL EXAMPLE

1. What do you think Esther's greatest fears were?

2. What is the most frightening challenge you have ever faced? What made it so scary?

3. What scary situation do you now face? What is at risk?

4. How might it be true that, just as with Queen Esther, God has brought you here "for such a time as this" (Est. 4:13–14)?

6. How did God supernaturally intervene in Esther's situation? When you find yourself in spiritual battle, what is God's responsibility? What is yours?

MY PRAYER

Lord, thank you for the challenge that I face today. Even though it is frightening, I will trust you with a heart that is willing to take a great risk on your behalf. Help me to understand why it is that you have brought me to this place. Empower me as I enter the battle. Show me what to do, I pray in Jesus' name and for his glory, amen.

CHAPTER THREE:
THE COURTSHIP OF GOOD AND EVIL

1. In what ways do you sense that you are the target of Satan's attacks?

2. How do you normally respond when Satan tempts or attacks you at your points of vulnerability? What typically happens?

3. Where is the Holy Spirit in relation to you when you are under Satan's attack? What is his role as your "Helper"?

4. The Bible refers to God as our Shield, Protector, Deliverer, Rock, Refuge, and Provider. How have you experienced this protection, deliverance, and provision of God in your life?

5. How would you *like* to experience those aspects of his character?

6. What does God's unconditional love for you look like? What does it mean for you to experience this kind of love?

MY PRAYER

Lord, you know the weaknesses of my life, and so does Satan. You have said that the Holy Spirit is my Helper. Help me, therefore, today to say "no" to those temptations that arise whenever I am feeling weak. I claim you as my Shield, Rock, Protector, Provider, and Refuge. Thank you for loving me, even in those times when I forget that you are with me. In Jesus' name and for his glory I pray, amen.

CHAPTER FOUR:
THE SPIRIT REALM

1. In what ways did Satan's attacks on your life change after you came to know Jesus Christ? What has Satan been trying to tell you?

2. Why is it that Satan continues to attack you, even though he knows you no longer belong to him?

3. At what points in your family history do you think Satan may have gained an entry point to harass subsequent generations, including you? What strongholds exist in your family that the enemy continues to exploit?

4. What choices have you made that provide a "foothold" in your life for the Devil? What do you need to do to eliminate that foothold?

5. Before we can ever hope to experience victory in spiritual battle, we must know where we ourselves stand. Do you have a real relationship with Jesus Christ? When did you accept him as your Savior? Identify the areas of your life where disobedience persists.

6. Have you "pledged your allegiance" to Jesus Christ and to follow him wherever he might lead? Take a moment in prayer to tell him you choose to serve him, and no other.

MY PRAYER

Lord, thank you for describing me as your very own daughter and princess. I realize that Satan's continuing attacks on my life simply mean that he is angry that he has forever lost me. You are aware of the strongholds that persist in my life. I choose today to renounce and forsake them, with a willingness to follow you wherever you lead, and to do whatever you direct. In Jesus' name, amen.

CHAPTER FIVE:
THE DYNAMICS OF BATTLE

1. Describe the way you see yourself. How do you think others see you?

2. Describe the way you see God. How do you think God sees you?

3. Describe the way you view men. How do you think men view you?

4. How is God allowing you to be tested by the Evil One? How might that testing actually be beneficial?

5. What will happen when you resist the Devil?

234 ENGAGING THE ENEMY

6. What are some negative core beliefs that you need to surrender to God so that He can change the way you think about men, women, and sex?

7. In what ways do you tend to justify or to minimize your favorite sins?

8. What are the dominant emotions you experience throughout a typical day? (Love, joy, awe, sorrow, fear, anger, jealousy, shame, disgust, pain, confusion, emptiness.) Where do those emotions lead you?

9. If you could picture and verbalize a bright future for yourself, what would that picture look like? How would you like God to use you?

10. In what area of your life is it most difficult to exercise faith?

11. What is the situation in your life that requires you to surrender your thoughts captive to Christ and to see the circumstances through God's compassionate, understanding, and loving eyes?

My Prayer

Lord, I recognize that the way I view myself and others is a distorted viewpoint. Help me to change the way I experience and interpret the actions, words, and even the nonverbal signals of other people. I surrender my thoughts to you and ask you to take them captive. Grant me a spirit of forgiveness for others who have hurt me. Banish unbelief from my heart and enable me to believe everything you have said. I pray in Jesus' name, amen.

CHAPTER SIX: DONNING OUR ARMOR

1. Describe what it means to be strong in Christ's mighty power (Eph. 6:10). How does that strength differ from your own?

2. Read Ephesians 6:13–18. What does it mean for you
   • to wear the belt of truth?

   • to wear the breastplate of righteousness?

   • to wear the "shoes" of the gospel?

   • to bear the shield of faith?

- to wear the helmet of salvation?

- to carry the sword of the Spirit?

3. What makes it difficult for you to have a consistent prayer life? What would help to facilitate a consistent prayer life?

4. Why does God tell us to pray? Describe in your own words what some of the effects of prayer are.

5. James 4:7 says, "Submit yourselves, then, to God. Resist the Devil, and he will flee from you." Explain what it means to submit to God. To resist the Devil?

6. How else does God provide protection for you? Has there ever been a time when you sense that God has been supernaturally protecting you? What do you think was happening?

7. What will enable you to become better skilled in using all the spiritual warfare weapons that God has made available to you?

MY PRAYER

Lord, thank you for the many blessings that you have lavished on my life. Protect me from the attacks of the Evil One as I grow to become more like Jesus. Remind me each day to put on your full armor and to remain in constant contact with you. I submit myself to you today and affirm that, with the help of your Holy Spirit, I will resist the Devil so that he will flee from me. Surround me with your hedge of protection and guard me by your holy angels. Continue to shape me into the skillful warrior you have called me to be. I pray in Jesus' name, amen.

CHAPTER SEVEN:
THE POWER OF THE TONGUE

1. Recall a compliment (spoken or written) that you have received. What impact did it have on your day?

2. What words would you like someone to say about you? Write yourself a note expressing the positive statement you have in mind.

3. Think about the way your prayers sound to God. Do you pray "if it is your will," about things that clearly *are* God's will? How do we know what God's will is? In what ways do you need to change the way you pray?

4. How can another person's free will affect the answers to our prayers? In what ways? Think of an example or two.

5. Psalm 66:18 says, "If I had cherished sin in my heart, the Lord would not have listened." Identify the areas in your life where you struggle to obey God. How might those areas of disobedience be weakening your prayers? What do you need to do?

6. God promises in Jeremiah 33:3 (NKJV) "Call to Me, and I will answer you, and show you great and mighty things, which you do not know." What are some great and mighty things you want God to show you? Pause, put this book down, and tell him about those things right now.

MY PRAYER

Father, thank you for seeing me as your daughter and princess. You have in many places in the Bible revealed your will to me. Help me to pray with discernment and in obedience so that your will might be done. Keep me from yielding to the temptations that would otherwise prevent me from seeing answers to my prayers. I rejoice in the precious promises you offer to me in your Word. Strengthen my faith so that I might personally experience their fulfillment. I pray in Jesus' name, amen.

CHAPTER EIGHT:
THE HOLY SPIRIT'S ROLE IN SPIRITUAL WARFARE

1. The author describes the Holy Spirit as our "breath." What would happen to us without the "breath of God"?

2. Many people can recall times when the Holy Spirit clearly seemed to be active in their lives. Describe such a time in your life when you powerfully sensed his presence.

3. The author writes, "… many uninformed believers tend to place the Holy Spirit in a box." What does she mean? How have you ever done that? What are some negative consequences of putting God in a box?

4. How have you sensed God speaking to you? What are some ways that God speaks to us? What are some misconceptions about discerning God's voice? How can we develop our ability to listen to God?

5. Read John 16:7, 13–14. Describe in your own words why Jesus gave the Holy Spirit to you.

6. What does it mean to grieve the Holy Spirit? What are some behaviors in which you engage that grieve Him?

7. In what ways do we flourish when we welcome the Holy Spirit's guidance?

My Prayer

Lord, I acknowledge that without your Holy Spirit I am lost and powerless. Thank you for the times you have spoken to me in your soft and gentle voice. Even before I was aware of your existence, you were drawing me to yourself. Forgive me for the times I allow distractions to stop me from actively listening to you. I invite you to speak to my heart today as you walk beside me. Help me to discern moment by moment your guidance for my life. Comfort, sanctify, and teach me today as I rely on you. I pray in Jesus' name, amen.

CHAPTER NINE: SATAN'S TACTICS

1. The author states that one of Satan's primary tactics is to turn believers against one another. Why is that true?

2. Describe a conflict with another believer that remains unresolved. How has that conflict affected your ministry and your walk with Christ? The ministry and walk of your fellow believer?

3. According to Proverbs 17:9, how should we respond when we hear negative information about another person? Why do we find it so difficult to do this?

4. Read Matthew 18:15–17. What should be the first and second steps toward resolving a conflict with a fellow believer? Why not simply send an e-mail to the other person?

5. Read Matthew 5:21–24. What if you sense you have offended another believer, what should you do? Why not wait until the other person works up the courage to approach you? After all, isn't it "their problem"?

6. In what ways have you recently experienced discouragement? Why is discouragement such an effective tool in Satan's hands? What is a possible solution to your discouragement?

7. What is the role of God's truth in frustrating the tactics of the Devil? Why is knowing God's Word essential to victory in spiritual battle?

MY PRAYER

Lord, thank you that in Christ the victory has already been won. I recognize that conflict between believers is a source of grief to you. Forgive me for the times I have been unwilling to resolve issues that have separated me from my fellow believer. Grant me the courage to approach that person and to restore our relationship. I also ask you to grant me a hunger for your Word so that I will base my life upon solid truth and not on the counterfeits that Satan brings my way. Dispel any sense of discouragement in my life so that I may walk in victory in the power of the Holy Spirit. I pray in Jesus' name, amen.

CHAPTER TEN:
PUSHING THROUGH THE OPPOSITION

1. Describe the battle in which you currently find yourself that seems as if it will never end.

2. Can you identify a sinful pattern—a generational curse—that you suspect has become ingrained in the spiritual blueprint of your family? What are the recurring struggles that you see among your grandparents, parents, siblings, and children? Whom do you need to forgive?

3. Why do ongoing generations continually struggle with generational curses? What is the role of *desire* in gaining deliverance? Are there any strongholds from which you truly do not desire deliverance? Identify them.

4. How has Satan used your need for approval to keep you under his control? How have others used your past against you?

5. Name the secret places in your life that you want to hide from God. What are the areas of sin that you suspect are too "big" for God to forgive?

6. Who are some people whom you trust to hold in confidence the areas of temptation and the strongholds with which you struggle? When will you call them to begin meeting together for the purpose of praying to tear down your strongholds and to break the generational curses that have captivated you?

MY PRAYER

Father, you know the sinful patterns that continue to plague my life. I rejoice that there are no sins in my life that are beyond the reach of your forgiveness. Help me now to forgive those who have in the past set in motion patterns of sin that are now wreaking such destruction in my life today. Motivate and strengthen me to shut doors of temptation. Free me from the need to gain the approval of other people. And thank you for the storms that you have allowed in my life. May they strengthen me to become a more powerful princess warrior. Grant me the courage to share my struggles with other sisters in Christ, to whom I will be able to disclose my secret places. Free me from the generational curses in my life, Lord. I pray in Jesus' name, amen.

CHAPTER ELEVEN:
SPIRITUAL WARFARE IN MARRIAGE

1. What are some character flaws that the people who know you best would identify in you? If you are married, what are some of the challenges you and your husband have repeatedly faced in your interactions?

2. The author wrote, "Forgiveness is not an invitation to another person to hurt us again." Identify some past experiences when you forgave your husband, and it seemed to invite more pain. How realistic is it to think that, once we offer forgiveness, we will not have to offer it again for the very same offense?

3. What happens when we refuse to forgive others? Think of a time when someone seemed to withhold forgiveness from you. How did it feel? What was the impact on your relationship?

4. Why is the concept of submission to a husband so difficult? For what reasons in your marriage do you find it difficult?

5. In what ways do you resist male leadership? Your husband's leadership? Why?

6. What comes to mind when you think of the term *feminism*? What are some differences between biblical womanhood and radical feminism?

7. Read Colossians 3:18. The word *submit* means "to place in an orderly fashion, to place under." Identify some biblical limits to a wife's obligation to submit. What are the differences between submission and abuse?

MY PRAYER

Lord, I am a flawed human being, but I realize and embrace the fact that you sent your Son to die for all my sins—past, present, and future. Help me to forgive my husband as repeatedly as you forgive me for my offenses against you. Speak to the wounded parts of my soul that make it difficult to honor his position in our family, a position that you have ordained. Keep my mind alert to the lies that our culture communicates about womanhood. Empower me to live as a godly example to my children. Shape me day by day into the helpmate for my husband that you have called me to be. I pray in Jesus' name, amen.

CHAPTER TWELVE:
SUFFERING AND SPIRITUAL WARFARE

1. According to the author, "Suffering is not always the direct result of sin," but is at times a natural *consequence* of our sinful behavior. What are some examples of natural consequences to decisions that you or people who are close to you have made?

2. Can you identify a sin for which there is *no* consequence?

3. What is the good of confessing a sin if we do not repent of it?

4. "Besetting sins," according to the author, "are usually present in our lives because of repeated behaviors that have ensnared us." Name one or two of your besetting sins. Then apply the "Five Rs"—Recognize, Renounce, Rebuke, Receive, and Rejoice—to that besetting sin.

5. Can you think of a sinful behavior or attitude from which you really do not desire healing? What happens if we do not desire release from a besetting sin? How should we pray for someone who does not want to give up such a sin?

6. What are some ways in which you have suffered due to the sinful behavior of someone else? Read Romans 8:28. How has God turned to good the action that someone else meant for evil? How might God do that in the future?

7. In what ways could God glorify himself through a situation that has brought you pain and discomfort?

8. How is the *way* we conduct ourselves in suffering even more important than the *why* of our suffering? Read Hebrews 2:10 and 5:8. How can suffering be beneficial?

9. Why do you think God seems never to allow us to reach maturity without a struggle? James 1:2–4 may offer some insight here.

My Prayer

Father, I am suffering at the present time. Some of it is due to my own behavior. But some of it is also due to the actions of other people. I really do want deliverance from my besetting sins. My choice today is to renounce the sin and to walk in freedom. I also ask you to give me your perspective as I endure and walk through this time of suffering. Glorify yourself and conform me to the likeness of your Son. I pray in Jesus' name and for his glory, amen.

Chapter Thirteen:
Dependency Outside of Christ

1. When we *enable* someone, we make possible or easier their dysfunctional, sinful, and inappropriate behavior. What are some ways that you *enable* others around you?

2. Why is it both unrealistic and sinful to expect our husbands to provide us with all the love and security we need? How is this a form of idolatry?

3. If you are in a codependent relationship, what were some of the unmet needs in your childhood that contributed to your current situation?

4. What are some of the consequences of codependency that you, or someone close to you, are experiencing?

5. Read the following verses and underline them in your Bible: Psalm 62:7–8; 1 Peter 5:7. Now personalize those verses and apply them to your own situation. In your own words, what do those verses tell you?

My Prayer

Lord, you know and understand my broken past. I confess to you the sin of idolizing that special person in my life. Thank you for your forgiveness. Help me now to shift my focus to you and you alone for strength and daily sustenance. Thank you for being the one person in whom I can trust to meet all my needs. I pray in Jesus' name and for his glory, amen.

Chapter Fourteen:
My Story of Warfare and Salvation

1. What are some ways in which the author's story resonates with your experience?

2. For what purpose do you sense that God has set you apart? What leads you to believe that?

3. Read 2 Corinthians 3:18. In what ways has the Lord changed you since you came to know Jesus Christ? How has your relationship with God changed your character and your view of the world?

4. Have there been times in your life when you have experienced what the author describes as an "arrested development," when your life seemed to be locked in immaturity? Describe such a time. What was it that hindered your growth?

5. How would you describe the process of discipleship you experienced after coming to salvation in Christ? What made the biggest difference in your life? What was missing?

6. Read the lyrics of "Warrior," which the author's brother penned. What in that song reflects your own experience and journey?

7. Having read *Engaging the Enemy*, how will you now approach the Christian life differently? What needs to change? What will be your first step?

MY PRAYER

Dear Lord, I praise you for coming to me when I was far away from you. You saw me and drew me to yourself and have called me both daughter and princess. You have had in mind a purpose for my life that is now just beginning to become clear to me. Help me to continue to feed on your Word, to walk in step with your Holy Spirit, and to grow into a mature follower of Jesus. Continue to change me from the inside out. Use the storms and the scars of my life to transform me into a wounded healer who will make a difference in the lives of those who are near and dear to me. I pray in Jesus' name and for his glory, amen.

Notes

CHAPTER 1

1. Adoption.com, "Adoption Statistics: Birth Family Search."
http://statistics.adoption.com/information/adoption-
statistics-birth-family-search.html.
2. Ralph Gower, *The New Manners and Customs of the Bible*
(Chicago: Moody Press, 1987), 65.

CHAPTER 3

1. Anne Fisher, "Stressed Out: Are We Having Fun Yet?" *Fortune*,
October 1996, 215.

CHAPTER 4

1. *NKJV Hebrew-Greek Key Word Study Bible* (Chattanooga, TN:
AMG International, 1996), Isaiah 14:13–14.

CHAPTER 5

1. Ed Murphy, *The Handbook for Spiritual Warfare* (Nashville: Nelson, 2003).
2. "The New Testament Lexical Aid," *NKJV Hebrew-Greek Key Word Study Bible* (Chattanooga, TN: AMG International, 1996).
3. Neil Anderson, *Christ Centered Therapy* (Grand Rapids, MI: Zondervan, 2000).
4. Robert Liardon, *Smith Wigglesworth; The Complete Collection of His Life Teachings* (Cincinnati, OH: Harrison House, 1997).

CHAPTER 6

1. *Genesis: An Expositional Commentary* (Grand Rapids, MI: Baker Books, 1998).

CHAPTER 11

1. "Notes From the First Year, Documents from the Women's Liberation Movement in the US," New York: The New York Radical Woman, 1968.
2. Ibid.
3. Ibid.
4. Americans for Divorce Reform. *Divorce Statistics Collection*, May, 2005.

CHAPTER 12

1. Andrew Murray, *The Believer's Prayer Life* (Minneapolis: Bethany House, 1983).
2. Ed Murphy, *The Handbook for Spiritual Warfare* (Grand Rapids, MI: Zondervan, 2003).